HOW TO BE A FILM PRODUCER

JOHN BURDER

Big Ben Books

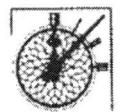

© Copyright John Burder 2015

First published by
BIG BEN BOOKS
2015

ISBN 978-0-9523890-9-5

All rights reserved. No part of this publication may be reproduced, stored in a retrieval system or transmitted in any form or by any means without the prior consent of the author.

HERE TODAY

WHERE TOMORROW?

HOW TO BE A FILM PRODUCER

CHAPTER ONE

It was six o'clock in the morning, and there we were. A twenty man film crew, with six actors, one rather bewildered actress, an ancient steam train and a veteran car - all marooned on a deserted railway track miles from anywhere. It had been raining all night and we were soaked to the skin but a brave attempt to appear cheerful united us all.

At the same time last week, we had driven across the Saudi Arabian desert in air conditioned vehicles to protect us from the heat of the sun. We were heading for another location - one we would be visiting every three months for the next two years. In those days, long before the advent of mobile phones and satellite navigation, we had driven through the night guided by a map on which we hoped we had correctly identified the point we needed to reach. When we eventually arrived, a blinding sandstorm quickly obscured everything and made it impossible to get out of our vehicles for a couple of hours.

The scene we were shooting on that rain-soaked railway line had taken us six months to set up.

When our film had been shot shot and edited it would be shown in cinemas around the world. Our final edited version would run for sixty seconds – the normal duration for many television and cinema commercials. It had started as an idea six months earlier. For several years I had been trying to persuade the makers of a leading brand of scotch whisky to let us make their advertising films.

My overtures had met with no success at all.

They were a huge and very successful multi-national company. We had been making films commercially for three years, though I had spent three more years at Ealing Studios and had also worked for the BBC. Their Advertising Manager - Charles Rusbridger – had managed his company's promotional efforts with considerable success for years and knew the business inside out.

I was in my twenties and, though I hoped he did not know it, he scared me to death. After months of making offers which were politely declined with a stereotyped letter explaining that the company appreciated our interest but was quite happy with its present suppliers, I knew I would have to do something different if we were to get anywhere. It was clear that the company needed films which could be used in different continents without a lot of costly dubbing. I also realised that, as their products sold very well in most of the markets they served they did not have an unlimited advertising budget.

I eventually managed to get them to agree that, if we could some up with an original idea and a realistic budget they would at least listen to what we had to say. After several sleepless nights and a lot of thought I came up with a storyline which hinged on someone stealing bottle of their finest whisky. I then added an old steam train and a veteran car to broaden its appeal and developed the theme to a point where I thought it might be interesting enough to appeal to our potential sponsor. After weeks more work that proved to be the case and we were given the green light to go ahead.

We had just four weeks to make it all work. Four weeks in which to find a suitable location, a cast of actors to perform and a host of period costumes and props ranging from an ancient steam train, with a driver and fireman, to a fully operational veteran car. It would have been quite a challenge for anyone but we were relatively new to the job and did not have the support of a big company to back us up. We knew success or failure was up to us.

Finding a suitable location to shoot our film had to be my first concern. Today, with heritage railway groups all over Britain, it would have been relatively easy but then, in the 1960s, not long after Doctor Beeching had closed many of the country's rural railway lines and scrapped hundreds of steam trains it was a much more complex task. I did some research and discovered that a group of railway enthusiasts had made a bid for a stretch of track which British rail had abandoned in rural Sussex, which they wanted to restore and reconnect with the two nearest towns. They had been attempting to raise a great deal of money for some time and had raised enough to buy a few miles of surviving track, a couple of small steam engines and a few coaches of various types. I went down to meet the people who were in charge of this pioneering work. They were full of enthusiasm and represented all that was good in Britain then and still is today. They wanted to keep Britain's heritage alive. When I explained what I wanted to do and asked if they felt they could help us to make our film they were interested and helpful. They explained that they only had limited resources. The track they had acquired and the trains that still worked were being restored and operated by volunteers who came from all walks of life. Students, retired railwaymen and people with many different skills, all played a part. The man who was to drive the train we eventually agreed to hire spent most of his life flying jumbo jets to Australia for a major British airline. On his off duty days he would escape from the cockpit and drive a ninety year old steam train up and down an equally ancient and very rusty track.

The volunteers were wonderful and they had great ambitions. Then - forty years ago - many thought they were attempting to do too much but, as I write these words, most of their ambitions have been achieved. Their venture is now called the Bluebell Line and it is a huge success. Inspired by their example, and the work of pioneers in other parts of the Britain, more heritage lines have been set up and key parts of our national heritage have been lovingly restored.

The success of our whisky commercial was good for business. It encouraged other sponsors to approach us to quote for making their films. It also ensured that our newly won and much courted client stayed with us. When they wanted another film they came to us without my having to write countless letters begging to see them We had established an excellent working relationship which lasted for many years. Like all relationships it had its ups and downs In those days big businesses worked in different ways to the ones they adopt now. A lot of business was done over lunch.

After the success of our train film I found that, when I was I asked to present ideas for another project,I was often invited to the board room for "a wee dram". The boardroom was at the heart of what was a very prestigious building. Portraits of the company's founders hung on oak panelled walls and priceless works of art were prominent elsewhere in the building. At the end of our discussions a button would be pressed and one of the founder's portraits would silently glide away revealing a small cupboard which was then carefully unlocked. It contained a small barrel of what was always referred to as "the product!" - The finest scotch whisky the company produced. There was another barrel alongside. It contained water from a highland spring near the company's distillery. My hosts were kind, generous and clearly interested in what we had achieved together.

On occasions, if things had gone particularly well, as I was preparing to leave and go back to my office one of my hosts would approach me and quietly whisper "A little lunch perhaps?" If I did not object, as they knew I never would, we would then adjourn to one of the he many excellent restaurants which were conveniently nearby. When we arrived we would always find a bottle of the company's best "product" had been placed on our table prior to our arrival.

 Alas, doing business in today's world is not the same at all! By now, as you may have gathered , my job does not involve commuting or normal office hours.

In those days a different atmosphere prevailed. I had the most important assets any child can have. Two loving parents, who were determined to overcome every disaster and get on with life. They were wonderful to me and everyone else they encountered and taught me the things that really matter in life. If had known then what I know now I would have loved them even more, if that were possible. As it was, my father was nearly seventy when I went to my first school. He had married a very beautiful and much younger wife when he was at quite an advanced age. As he would never talk about his early life, it took me sixty years to find out more and begin to understand the father who, when I was young, I discovered I hardly knew. When I was born he was the Rector of a small country parish. I knew he had been ill before I was born. The family had moved from Huntingdon - the county town where dad had been Rector of St Mary's parish church, to a smaller parish because he had been too ill to cope with a larger one, No one told me why. My father did everything anyone could have done to make me happy and give me a good life but there was one subject which in our house was ever mentioned. No one discussed the war. As a child I assumed that was because of my brother's death. Mum and Dad had been to Buckingham Palace to collect his Military Cross. They came home and put it away in a drawer. Nothing else was ever said . Dad never mentioned his own experiences in the first world war, for which he too had been awarded a Military Cross.

71 years later, long after my father's death, when I was clearing out the house I then lived in, I came across an old cabin trunk. It had been moved from house to house over the years but had never been opened. When I undid the straps which held it together, I found it contained the handwritten manuscript of a book which my father had written when he returned from the trenches in 1918. It was a vivid first hand account of the four years he had spent under fire which had ended when he was seriously wounded in battle at Ypres.

The Sun newspaper got hold of an advance copy and wrote a two page feature about it. As a result of that exposure the first hardback edition sold out in three weeks. My father's words were reprinted as a paperback. I also recorded an abridged audio book version. Doing all these things I began to realize how little I knew of the astonishing life my father had lead,.and how many opportunities I had missed because I did not know his book was there.

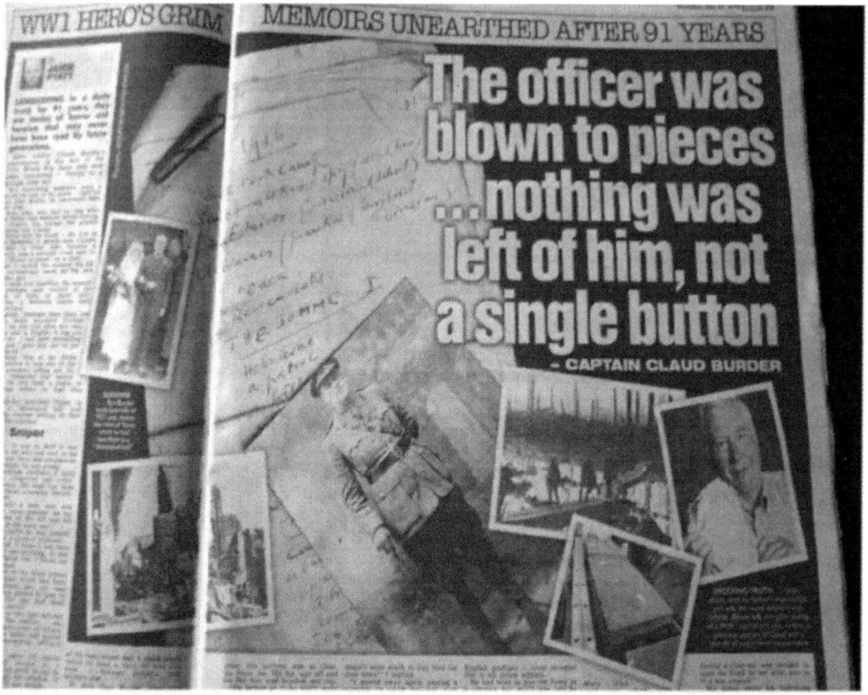
WW1 HERO'S GRIM
MEMOIRS UNEARTHED AFTER 91 YEARS
The officer was blown to pieces ...nothing was left of him, not a single button
- CAPTAIN CLAUD BURDER

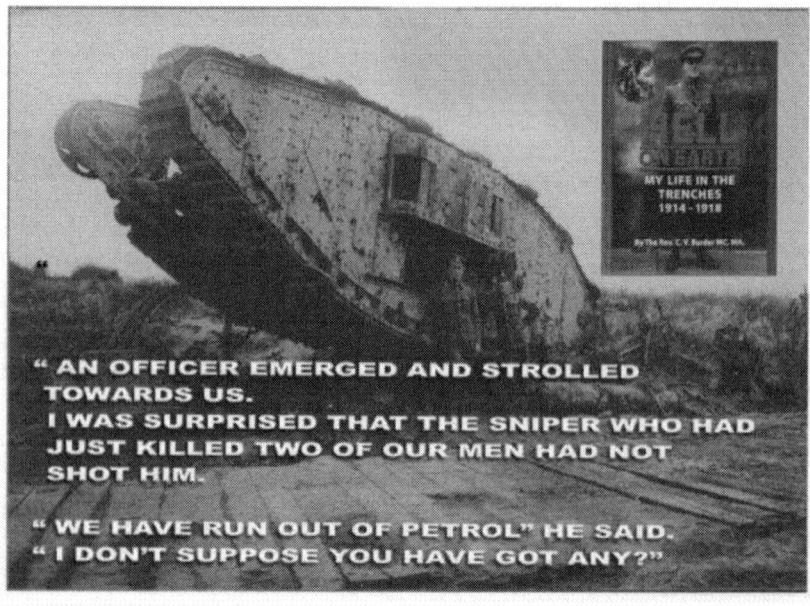

MY LIFE IN THE TRENCHES 1914 - 1918
" AN OFFICER EMERGED AND STROLLED TOWARDS US.
I WAS SURPRISED THAT THE SNIPER WHO HAD JUST KILLED TWO OF OUR MEN HAD NOT SHOT HIM.
" WE HAVE RUN OUT OF PETROL" HE SAID.
" I DON'T SUPPOSE YOU HAVE GOT ANY?"

Unaware of anything which had taken place between 1914 and 1918 I grew up in the country as world war two approached its end. In 1946 I went to my first school. It was a girls school, the pleasures of which I was a bit too young to appreciate then. I can only recall that the teacher in charge of my class was a Miss Silver who I seem to recall was kind though I was so terrified when I first arrived that I peed all over the floor, which probably wasn't the best way of making the right impression.
Today Slepe Hall is a popular hotel but then it was my first step away from home and big adventure.
From there as I got older I was sent to a prep school which had been moved from the Kent coast during the war, when it was thought to be in danger of being hit by shellfire from German forces across the English channel. It was run by Benedectine monks who had their own ways of doing things.
In many ways it was good and the standard of teaching was generally high but it was run on very strict lines the likes of which would not be allowed today.
As we were constantly reminded, rules were rules and they must be obeyed. If we were evil enough to run in a corridor or be late for class our names would be written in the headmaster's little black book. After tea each day the names he had noted would be read out and the boys concerned would line up outside the head's study. They were then called in one by one and caned very hard indeed. In those days that kind of treatment was considered normal. I got used to having a sore bottom and worked hard to avoid being thrashed again, so I think it probably did me good.
It was at that school that I took another step along the road that would eventually lead me to a life in films.

From time to time at the end of the school day we
would be shown a film. The assembly hall was specially
prepared for the occasion. Its walls were lined with
clothes lockers but for film shows rows of chairs were
imported from classrooms. Staff sat in the chairs and
we sat on the lockers while a screen was set up and the
first 16mm film projector I had seen was produced from
its box. The atmosphere was electric and when the first
title appeared on the screen the air was
filled with the cheers and shouts of a hundred boys
letting off steam.
The films we saw were carefully selected and generally
quite up to date. One of the first I can recall was
MRS MINIVER which had recently been released after
after winning several awards. On one occasion I shall
not forget the film was preceded by a live performance
in which a boy was beaten in front of the whole school.
I cannot recall what Tom had done but vividly remember
him being made to bend over a table in front of all the
boys and staff and receiving twelve strokes of the cane
which our headmaster - Father Edward - delivered very
hard indeed. We were all shocked, and left wondering
who would be next. The film which followed his live
performance was *BOYS TOWN* - an MGM classic in
which Spencer Tracy played a benevolent priest who
helped boys who were in trouble. His Oscar winning
performance was hard to appreciate after what we had
just seen.
Many years later, when I had left school and was living
and working in London, I decided I would like to
visit my old school. The people I remembered had
long since gone and the school had moved from it's
temporary wartime location back to Ramsgate in Kent
which is where it had been before the war. Father
Edward and his staff had all left and the school was very

different to the setup I recall. I decided to make a few enquiries and asked if anyone knew what had happened to the staff I had known. When I asked the church authorities I got little or no response. No one remembered anything and if they did, they were not telling me. I found their attitude difficult to understand and wanted to find out more. I eventually discovered that Father Edward and his "housekeeper", who had been with him when he was Headmaster of the school, had moved to a seaside town in Kent where he had become the Parish Priest. They were living together in quite a large house and it was there that one night they were murdered by a man who, it transpired later, was known to have had mental health issues. When their bodies were found enquiries began and I due course a suspect was arrested and charged. From that point on official records have have proved difficult to access and I still do not know the details of the case. I have been left with a feeling that there may be something which someone does not want us to know. My only thought is that it is was a sad end for a man who had many good points . He taught me a lot.

When my father died and I myself prepared to retire. I had to sort out his papers. Among them I found a letter which Father Edward had written to my father when I had left school.

It was attached to my last school report. In it he said how proud my father should be with the progress I had made and how confident he was that I would be a success in life.

In school holidays I helped my parents with their parish duties and explored the surrounding countryside on a battered bike. In those days, before computers and mobile phones, we had to make our own entertainments. Climbing trees, walking for miles through unspoiled country and observing the oddities of village life were all ways having a good day.

  Our village was small and those who lived there generally worked on the land. Until RAF Wyton had been built just before the war there were few other ways of earning a living but it's the characters I met and not the places I visited that I tend to recall. Living in a small country parish was certainly quiet but it was never dull. As the vicar's son I was expected to attend church at least once a week and that was always more entertaining that it was ever meant to be. On Sundays the church, which had been built to accommodate hundreds of rich landowners in earlier days, usually welcomed a congregation of three. There was Mrs Webb - the Vicar's Warden, who was rather deaf and used to join in the hymns and prayers about half a verse after anyone else who happened to be there. Her efforts were supported by Mrs Green (The Peoples' Warden) who would never be outdone on volume. My father acted as a kind of referee and tried to cope with a situation which would have put anyone else in an early grave. It was country life in the 1950s at its very best and I am very glad I was able to be there.

My mother, who had to cope with running our enormous rectory and deal with most of the social affairs of the parish, was the nearest to a saint I shall ever meet. The family's total income of around £500.00 a year was a derisory sum even then but she would never be deterred. When disasters happened, as they did quite often, she always managed to smile and adopt a frame of mind which made it seem as if the Christian life she had chosen to adopt was as full of joy as the scripture proclaimed.

Visiting sick parishioners was one of the duties she felt she should perform. On most occasions that meant going to see people who the rest of the world preferred to forget It was s gesture which was not always appreciated and one which sometimes produced unexpected results.

Mirabelle Clifton lived alone in a large house at the top of a hill. Her overgrown garden backed on to the local aerodrome. During the war Ms Clifton had created a stir by complaining that RAF pilots on their way to Germany were flying round her house watching her undress. When the war ended she boarded up her windows and became a recluse. From time to time she opened a door wide enough for food to be passed through but otherwise made no contact with the outside world.

My mother became concerned about her health and decided we ought to pay her a visit.
We arrived at the isolated house as the sun was setting. The windows were boarded up and a warning that trespassers would be prosecuted was nailed to the door. Plucking up courage my mother stepped forward and knocked on the door. At first there was no response but eventually we heard a voice.
" Go away! You are not wanted".
" It's only me - Mrs Burder. The vicar's wife" my mother replied. For a long time there was silence then, just as we were about to move away, we heard locks being unbolted and mutterings from within.
Eventually the door was opened but there seemed to be nobody inside. Then we heard a voice. "Come in and don't dawdle. I haven't got all day"! We did as we were told and immediately the door was slammed and bolted behind us. There was almost no light inside and a very unpleasant smell. We stood there transfixed and then we heard a voice from the shadows.
"I'm here" she said from a small room at the end of a corridor which was piled high with boxes. As we moved forward she drew back the one remaining curtain and dust flew in all directions. In the centre of the room an upturned crate was the main attraction. A few old car seats stood nearby and in an ancient fireplace a kettle was balanced on the remains of a fire. Two cups and a teapot rested on the crate. Mirabelle moved from the curtain to a cupboard." Tea?" She enquired. Before we could reply she opened the cupboard and took out a tin. There was a picture of the King on top of the lid. My mother tried to make polite conversation as Mirabelle opened the tin and tipped some white powder into the pot. Water was added without another word. As the kettle was returned to the hearth my mother looked at me. Her eyes said it all. They expressed fear and despair but what could be done? There were no potted plants we could pour the liquid into and every move we made was being watched. Drawing strength from her unquenchable religious faith, my mother picked up a cup. I had visions of being orphaned there and then.

She told me later that she was convinced her last minute had come. Fortunately it had not. The powder turned out to be bicarbonate of soda!

As we prepared to leave I think we felt that, in spite of everything, our visit had been a success. But what did Ms. Clifton feel about what for her must have been quite a special occasion? As she closed the door and started to fasten rows of bolts she delivered her verdict. " You have been very kind" she said, And I am not one to forget an act of kindness. I shall come along and see you in church."

It was a promise we did not expect her to keep but we were wrong. Two weeks later the congregation at evensong swelled to four as Mirabelle kept her promise. Her arrival was impossible to miss.

In an attempt to scare off any evil spirits which might attack her as she walked through the village, she had tied all the saucepans she possessed on a string round her waist. As she arrived at church alone, the precaution seemed to have worked!

When I was not taking tea with my father's parishioners, I spent my free time exploring the attractions of the villages which I could reach on my bike. Until my father retired we never had a car. My mother, who had learned to drive in the war, then bought an very old car (A Standard 8). If it started at all it usually broke down after a mile or so. It was eventually replaced with an even older Ford which produced clouds of blue smoke which came up through the floor. Until I left my last school and started looking for a job I travelled on two wheels. First on a series of battered bikes and then on a Francis Barnett 75cc auto cycle was nearly twice as old as me. It had a back pedal brake which was great when it worked and it gave me the freedom to explore roads which in those days in the country were often traffic free.

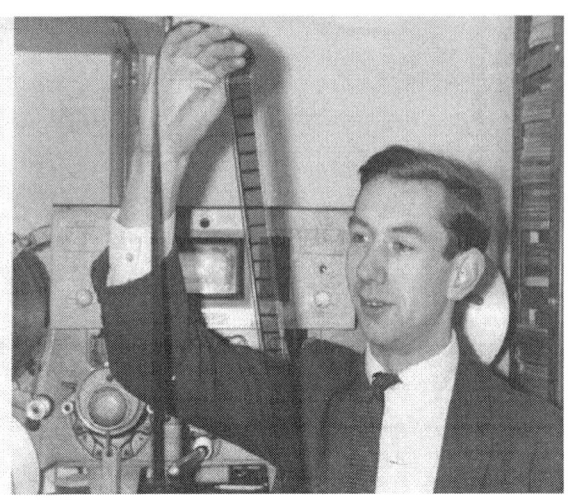

When I got my first job I was able to buy a BSA Bantam motorcycle , which was my pride and joy for many years. It was new and reliable and allowed me to travel further afield, Huntington and St Ives - the towns nearest home - had been good for a time but now the attractions of Cambridge were just half an hour away. At eighteen years of age a new chapter had begun.

When I was not in the Arts cinema in Cambridge, The Hippodrome in Huntingdon or The Regal in St Ives I was was usually to be found reading books or magazines about films and the cinema. I was also beginning to get interested in how films were made. My favourite cinema in my youth was the Huntingdon Hippodrome. Now alas long gone, it had its own character and charm. I spent many happy hours watching the big stars of the day on the Hippodrome screen. Peter Ustinov giving his Oscar winning performance as Nero in *QUO VADIS*.. David Niven going *AROUND THE WORLD IN 80 DAYS* - the Mike Todd film for which he too won an Oscar. Vincent Price, scaring me to death in X rated Hammer horror films which I was not legally old enough to see. Little did I know then that a few years later I would be directing the stars I admired then in films which would be shown around the world.

At the Hippodrome they did their best to put on a professional performance. Russ Conway records tinkled away as we entered. At the appointed hour lights would dim and, as curtains rose a slide would flash across the screen. It informed us that "This cinema is disinfected daily with San Izal." After that world shattering news the curtains would close and Ice cream tubs and choc bars would be served by "the lady with the tray" who was usually at least twice the age of the attractive blondes who appeared in the ice cream advertising films which preceded her arrival. A cartoon, newsreel and the main feature followed then audiences raced for the doors to get out before the National Anthem was played. I sat there transfixed. To me at 13 it was a magical world but more important things were waiting in the wings. I knew I would soon have to go to new school. My parents original idea has been to send me to Canford school in Dorset, where my brother had done well. After he was killed, a few weeks after joining the army when he left school, I think they thought the memories that might rekindle could prove too much. And there was another factor they had to consider. My father was in his seventies and struggling to remain fit enough to continue his work as a parish priest. He was a man who would never give up and would always do what he felt was right but his war wounds were taking their toll, as they had since he came back to England in 1918. There was another problem too. Church of England clergy are not paid a fortune . We lived in a large rectory but we did not own it. It had to be maintained and we were very short of cash. That was why we did not have any of the modern comforts everyone today takes for granted. Nothing was ever said but I knew my father was looking round for a good school which he could afford to so I could complete my education. At about this time he met a friend he had been at school with himself many years before. They had kept in touch over the years and my father's contemporary had also gone into the church in his later years. Unlike my dad he had never married. He had also inherited a great deal of money from a relative .

I was taken to Bournemouth to be introduced. I remember our first meeting and I am not proud of my performance. My father's friend looked like the old man he clearly was. Unlike dad, who was always joking and enjoyed life to the full, his friend was dressed entirely in black. Perched on his head was an ill fitting wig which looked like a dead cat. The effect was bizarre and I don't think I can have reacted very well.

Many years later, just before my father died, I heard what that visit had produced. My father's friend had heard about a new public school which was about to open a few miles away. The man behind the new venture was another cleric - The Rev Dr C.K. Francis Brown, who had started and run a successful prep school in Surrey. He had agreed to take over Milton Abbey - a stately home 8 miles from Blandford in Dorset. It had been a faith healing centre until the company's bankers had run out of faith. Since then its had been unoccupied so the proposed new school would be starting from scratch with just 25 boys. If My father and I liked what was being proposed. His friend would pay my school fees for five years. It was a very a generous offer and one my father could not afford to refuse. Three weeks later Dad and I found ourselves in Dorset touring the building which was to become a school in just a few weeks. Dr Brown was not an easy man to get to know. As his track record shows he was good at starting schools but not so good at running them. In the course of his career he started Woolpit school in Surrey, Milton Abbey in Dorset, and two other successful schools. He had a few disasters but generally the schools he started did well when he moved out. I went to see him several years after I had left school and started my first job. He looked much as he had done when I had first met him. He was about to open another school. This time it was to be a sixth form college near Oxford.. He was as self assured and pompous as he had always been but there was something in his manner which did not seem right. A few weeks after that meeting, one night when everyone was out, he drove his car into a garage, fixed a long hose to the exhaust pipe and left the engine running. His body was found the following day.

On my first visit to Milton Abbey, three weeks before it became a school, my father and I were told by Dr Brown that he planned to make it "The Eton of the west". Fortunately that never happened but the concept was typical of the man. Full of pompous ideas and some very good ones, but without enough money to make them work. Today Milton Abbey is a first class school but its first few years were a real test of faith and hope. It could never happen now. Today there are too many laws and restrictions affecting any new business to make setting up a venture that size, with next to nothing, impossible to even contemplate. Dr Brown was a man of faith and he managed to persuade a handful of backers to support his ideas. He also recruited good staff who rallied to the cause. Gradually what many had dismissed as a hopeless task began to take off.

I was at Milton Abbey when the school first opened. In 2015, as I write these words, I am just stepping down as President of the Milton Abbey Association. I am now 75 and its time for a younger person to take over. Today Milton Abbey is a huge success. It is not a big school. That is one of its main attractions. It is small enough to give young people the individual care and attention they need when they are starting out in life.

I owe a lot to Milton Abbey. It was there that I was finally able to decide what I wanted to do in life and it was there that I produced my very first film. My housemaster - Michael Charles - a six foot tall Historian who stood and walked at an angle which reminded me of the leaning tower of Pisa - owned a very old movie camera - a Cine Kodak Model B. It was powered by a clockwork motor and he very generously lent it to me. I recruited a few like minded guys and we called ourselves the Milton Film Unit. Our aims were simple. We set out to film anything which moved and to try and record what life in the school at that time was all about. Making that very amateur film was to change my life. When fully wound up, our camera would run about 30 seconds of film thorough its very basic mechanism. There was a fixed focus wide angle lens and very little else. It was one step up from a pretty basic toy but, to a thirteen year old boy who had never seen a movie camera before, it was a gift from God.

THE ORIGINAL MILTON FILM UNIT

When you have never made a film before, and find yourself handling a movie camera for the very first time it can be quite bewildering. When you are 13 years old you are fairly used to trying new things but making movies requires a lot of different skills and I suppose that is what appealed to me. I have spent my life trying to acquire those skills and I am still learning. If you have made a school film or any amateur home movie you will know what I mean. If you are reading this book and thinking you might like to work in films you will soon discover what a lot there is to learn. As a film maker you need to learn about writing and reading scripts. As you will be working with sounds and pictures you will need to have at least a basic knowledge of how both can be recorded, edited and used most effectively to make your script work. That can take years but you can start, as I did, reading books and then borrowing a camera and conducting your own experiments to find out what you need to do and how everything works. In our school film we set out to show what Milton Abbey at that time was all about. We started without a script and we quickly realised that we were going to have to film a lot of different events and visit lots of different places at different times of year to tell the story we wanted to put across. So in stead of a script we started with a list of events, dates and locations. That helped us to narrow the subject down and only shoot scenes we were likely need to tell make our film. As our shot list got longer we started to think how the shots we proposed to film could be used to link one subject to another. Those links would eventually form the basis of a commentary script.

The film was actually shot over a number of years, I and some of the other 25 boys who arrived on the school's first term started it off. When we left we had a an edited version which ran for about ten minutes. When we went into the world to earn a living others took over and so what was always described simply as "the school film" continued to be produced. Everyone who worked on it over the years managed to learn something and to have a lot fun in the process. Several later decided to look for careers in what is now generally referred to as "the media" and have had considerable success.

As time passed the film recorded the development of the school. Headmasters came and went. At one point the school caught fire and one wing was completely destroyed. New buildings appeared and old ones were restored, Where there had only been basic facilities, the school added a theatre, an indoor swimming pool and lots of other things which we as pioneers would love to have had.

Several years after I had left, when I had become a television Producer and was working for the BBC, I brought some of my colleagues to the school and we spent four very hectic weeks bringing the film up to date. It has recently been updated again to mark the school's 50th anniversary and a Royal visit. Digitally restored copies on are now available on DVD, so story of Milton Abbey's first fifty years remains very much alive.

FROM THE ARCHIVES

MILTON ABBEY SCHOOL - 1995

When the time came for me to leave school I had hoped to follow my father to Christ's College Cambridge but it was not to be.
I did not have his brains and , while I had been in my last year at school he had decided to retire. That meant that, when he stepped down, we would be homeless. The rectory which had been home   to our family for the over   forty years would be taken over by my my father's successor. It was clear that I had to get a job to support myself and my parents in their retirement.
We were in the 1950s. The war years had   passed.   In 1953 confectionery rationing ended and chocolate appeared in the shops for the first time since I was born. I remember being very sick after enjoying my first experience of chocolate peppermint creams. Things were looking up but it was still difficult to buy clothes, find a home or get a job. Mum and Dad moved to a small house in Brighton. I wanted to go to London as many young people do but I knew that my first priority had to be getting a job which would earn me enough to pay the bills. I knew what I wanted to do but as, I had only Just left school and only had limited qualifications I did not expect employers to rush out and greet me with open arms.
At school I had finally realised that I wanted to make films and thought, if I leaned more I might stand a chance of   building a career.
Unfortunately   I was not alone.   As I was soon to find out, thousands of others had the same idea. Some were attracted by what they thought was glamour. They saw themselves   on vast film sets, surrounded by pretty girls   looking   butch and shouting "Cut"!   Others thought they were born to become mega-stars. Cary Grant could not go on for ever and then they would have their chance.
Fortunately   my ambitions were less more down to earth, I had fallen in love with the crafts involved in making films.

I had enjoyed finding out how cameras work and seeing how creative lighting can transform a scene. The power professional film makers have to present and influence images and decisions had been revealed to me and it had interested me very much. While I waited for a suitable door to open I went back to school - this time to teach.

It was an absurd idea . I was just nineteen and had left school a few weeks before after failing almost every exam I faced. But one fact was clear, I needed a job, So when I was asked if I would stand in for a teacher who was sick. I accepted the challenge and hoped it would work out. For a term, I taught English and French to boys whose ages ranged from 13
to a few weeks younger I was myself. I think I learned more than they did from me. In the sixth form two of the boys were French. As they had spoken their native tongue since they had been born, my attempts to hold their interest for more than a few seconds were doomed to failure.

When I was not trying to teach I passed my time writing letters. I had spent hours listing the names of companies I wanted to join. All the big names were there. The owners of film studios and cinema chains. Television and radio companies. Independent Producers and firms that had produced the films I had seen at school. The letters went out and I sat back and waited for a response. It was a long wait but eventually a slow trickle of replies did start to arrive. Those who bothered to reply were obviously nice helpful people. They all thanked me for my letter and my interest in their work. And they all regretted that they did not have any suitable vacancies at the moment but promised they would keep my letter on file. Years later, when I was running a production company myself, I used to receive hundreds of letters like the ones I once wrote. I tied to answer them all but, when computers and E mails made it easy for anyone to write to everyone I had to give up and just hope that the people who were waiting for good news would eventually find what they were looking for, as I did when I had almost given up hope.

My salvation came from an unexpected quarter I had known of their existence for quite a long time. At school, when I formed

The Milton Film Unit, it occurred to me that it might be a good idea to have film shows, as they had done at my at prep school, so we could see how it ought to be done. I did some research and found the names of a number of firms which specialised in the distribution of films to what were officially described as "shut in locations". That meant hospitals, prisons and schools like mine. One of those distributors was a film library which was owned by the Rank Organisation. We all knew that J Arthur Rank was one of the most powerful men in the British film industry. He owned all the Odeon and Gaumont cinemas. Pinewood Studios and a host of companies which processed films and made equipment for the film and television industries were also controlled by him. The film library which had supplied the films we saw at school was part of his empire, so I thought I might try dropping him a line.

As I did not have a job there was nothing to lose. My schools had all been customers of his for years so I hoped the mighty Rank empire might welcome me with open arms. On this occasion, much to my surprise, in due course I did get reply. My letter had been passed to the man who was in charge of the film library I had mentioned, which fortunately I had praised. He now wrote to thank me for my interest. He ended by saying that, if I made an appointment with his secretary, he would be pleased to show me how things were done.

I knew Rank films always started with shot of a man with a gong and had read about Pinewood, Hollywood and lots of major stars , but knew almost nothing else. Ranks had kindly sent me a map which showed the location of the place I was to visit. It was twenty minutes walk from Ealing Studios, which Rank did not own, where they were producing many of Britain's finest films. I followed my instructions and eventually arrived at a two storey 1930s office block opposite a factory which made Hoover washing machines. There was a cafe next door which was called "Jox Box". Hollywood it as not! I made my presence known and was eventually welcomed by the man who had responded to my letter. I was 19. He was in his forties, but he made me feel welcome and was good at his job. We chatted for an hour. He asked lots of questions and I explained how I had

dealt with his company when I was at school. Then I casually mentioned that I was hoping to get into the film industry and was looking for a job. I was surprised to find that he knew all about me. Ranks had done their research and written to my school. They knew about the Milton Film Unit and had probably anticipated the question I asked. He then explained that they were only concerned with film distribution. Production was handled by a different division and, if that is what I wanted to do, I would have to speak to them. As he had promised, he showed me round. As I prepared to leave the he told me that, if I did not get anywhere with my production ambitions, I could always come back and take a temporary job on his staff while I continued to look around. That sounded like a great idea to me and, a couple of weeks later, that is what I did.
When my father finally retired we had to leave the rectory in which I had been born and had lived ever since. Dad found a small house in Brighton. I thought it was awful but, as it was near the sea and easy to keep clean my mother loved it.
Before I could start work I had to find somewhere to live in London. As I could not afford a house or a flat I started to look round for somewhere I could rent. I managed to find a small bed sitting room in a large Victorian house in an unfashionable part of Ealing. It was about the size of one of the the lavatories in the house I which I was born but it was clean and cheap. Breakfast was included and the house was near Ealing Broadway station, so it was easy to escape to the West End, where there were around fifty cinemas and theatres all of which were grander and more expensive than the Huntingdon Hippodrome.

My new home was twenty minutes walk across a park to my new job with the Rank Organisation. On the day I was due to start work I wore by newly acquired Rank tie, on which the man with the gong was prominently displayed, and set out to meet my new colleagues. For the first time in my life I set foot in an open plan office, where around fifty people worked from nine o'clock each morning five days a week, I would have felt equally at home landing on the moon.

In my first week I started to learn who everyone was and what they did. The building housed several different departments, all of which were treated as empires by the people who ran them. There was Bookings, Accounts and Despatch and a number of partitioned off areas where managers and would be managers could doze off without being watched. There was also a canteen which served undrinkable tea in working hours and a meal mid day. That meant fish and chips on Fridays and pie an chips or something equally exotic the rest of the week. For five shillings we could have a three course lunch. It would start with soup of the day. Pie or fish would follow and the climax would be a dessert. Fruit salad (tinned) and ice cream or rice pudding were often on the list. Tea or coffee, made with Camp Coffee Essence, was an optional extra which some found was hard to resist.

On Friday nights the canteen was used for a staff film show. Free of charge, we were able to watch the latest West End releases which we distributed to ships at sea and other "shut in locations".The shows were principally an excuse for the girls who worked in bookings to sit in the back rows with their boy friends from despatch, without being observed by the parents with whom most of them still lived. As I mentioned before, it was not like Hollywood but, as the first full time job for a man who was now twenty years old, it it was a unique experience which I would hate to have missed. As I got used to my new surroundings I began to be accepted as part of the team.

I started to appreciate what the company did and I learned quite a lot. We distributed entertainment features and commercially sponsored documentary and promotional films to industry and the specialist locations I have already mentioned. We also had a small department which dealt with industrial training films.

I was able to observe how departments were run, what titles were in demand and how our customers needs were or weren't being met. Years later, when I was running an independent production company, the observations I made at that time stood me in good stead and helped me to increase our company's profits in a number of key areas.

When I joined Ranks I had expected the business would be managed by Arthur Rank himself. I was as naïve as that! It took me less than an hour to learn that my boss rarely visited the companies he owned. When he did it was the studios and larger parts of his empire he chose to see. Day to day business and the success of the company depended of his management team. At the head of that team was my boss - John Davis. An accountant by trade and one of most ruthless and disliked Managers I was to encounter in the course of my career.

He delegated power to a limited extent. Pinewood studios was nominally run by Earl St John - a mild mannered American who did what he as told.

Our film library had a Manger who had managed to show a profit for long enough to avoid a VIP visit though I was told he had looked in for an hour or two in days gone by. My only experience of his management style was the outcome of of a dinner he had hosted at the Dorchester hotel.

All the high and mighty had gathered there for the presentation of some awards.. At one table Davis sat with members of his Board of Directors and VIP guests. Across the room, in another prominent position there was a table for Rank's top stars. Many of the actors and actresses I had worshipped on the screen were there, all having a very good time. One of those present was Kenneth More. He was then at the height of his fame. GENEVIEVE, NORTHWEST FRONTIER, and A NIGHT TO REMEMBER had made millions for the company and at that time he was probably their biggest star name. As the dinner neared its end Davis stood up to make a speech. More, who was expecting to hear his name being announced as the star of major epic which was soon to go into production, had been celebrating the announcement with his actor friends. As Davis got into his speech Kenny, who was a very nice man who would not harm anyone, decided to join in. In a voice boosted with booze he heckled Davis from across the floor. The speech went on and on, and so did Kenny. Davis's remarks were punctuated with a barrage of inappropriate remarks. Davis continued until he had finished everything he had intended to say.

The following day More went to Rank's head office to apologise and, he hoped, to find out when work on his new film was going to start. In stead he was told that his contract had been terminated. He never worked for Rank again. As they controlled most of the UK's leading production and distribution companies, and many of the country's cinemas, other employers would not work with More. In the years which followed he made a few minor films for independent Producers but he had effectively ended his career.

My own departure from the Rank organisation took place later. It was my decision to leave and my departure was unannounced.

In my morning paper I had noticed a small advertisement on an inside page. It was just a few lines in small type and I was later told that it only appeared once but it was to change my life. It was advertising a BBC television training Course. It would take three year to complete and when it ended those taking part would be offered a full time job on the staff of the BBC. An interest in photography, sound recording or editing were considered desirable .

I read the advertisement several times, dreamed about it overnight and sent in off a request for an application form. It arrived a couple of weeks later. It took me several days to provide the information it required. After the last page of questions there was a note inviting applicants to to add any additional information they wished to provide in two blank sections on the back of the form. I could have written volumes. The course represented all I had hoped for and tried to find for months.

In stead I simply stated what I had done when we made our school film and why I wanted to know more. The
form was then sent off and I started what seemed to me to be a very long wait. Two months later, when I had almost given up hope ad was convinced my application form and been lost in the post, a small brown envelope arrived. Thinking it was just another bill I set it aside and cooked my breakfast As I had planned to go out for the day I thought I had better see how much the bill was for, as it could affect the amount I could spend that day. In stead of a bill I found a very brief letter. It thanked me for submitting my application form and apologised for the delay in acknowledging its receipt. That was reassuring. At least now I knew they had got it. It was the last few lines which came as a surprise.

They read - "Your application has been short listed and you are asked to attend for an interview at this address on the date shown below. Your interview is scheduled to start at 11 am. If for any reason you are unable to attend please contact the undersigned well in advance of your interview date". For the first time in my life I could not believe my eyes. It was all beyond my wildest hopes.

By the date of the interview I had come down to earth. Reality had taken control. I just knew that I had to find a presentable shirt and tie and report to a BBC office opposite Broadcasting House where I would face a barrage of questions from lots of people I had never heard of or met. I did not know who they would be or what they might ask, so all I could do was pray that all would be well, and that is what I did, as I have throughout my life.

I arrived on time looking reasonably smart and reported to reception. I was not alone. Twenty people were being interviewed that day. The Chairman of the interviewing committee introduced his colleagues who sat together at one long table. He apologised for the delay in processing my application and explained that there were five places on the training scheme and they had received letters from over over two thousand applicants!

The interviewing team consisted of the Chairman, who had been a radio announcer until he had decided to switch to a more secure job in the BBC Establishment Department. There was a television Producer, the Head of the Training and a Technical Manager from the Film Department.. There was also a middle aged lady in an large flowered hat who seemed to be asleep through most of the proceedings.

They did their best to put me at ease and after a while I started to relax.

They asked what I had done at school and why I wanted to get into television. I did not dare tell them that at home we did not even have a television set. They had done their homework and had followed up the references I had provided. They assured me that they had all been supportive. The lady with the hat finally woke up and asked me what newspaper I had read that morning. I named the paper the position I was applying for had been advertised in. She nodded and then seemed to doze off again, so I think my answer was probably correct.
Eventually the Chairman wound up the proceedings and I went home, convinced that I had no hope at all of getting a job. It had all been far too relaxed. There had been laughter and we had got on well. With so many people and so few jobs, I was convinced I did not stand a chance.

For several weeks I heard nothing. As I had left the Rank organisation and was unemployed I needed to earn some money so I started to look around. It as just before Christmas that the bombshell arrived. I was away visiting friends. When I got home I found a pile of letters. The first one I opened was short and clear. It simply stated the facts. After thanking me for attending a recent interview it explained that I had been selected for one of the posts I had applied for. I was instructed to report to Ealing Studios at 09.03am on a date which was three weeks away . For the first time, a life in films seemed to be firmly on the cards.

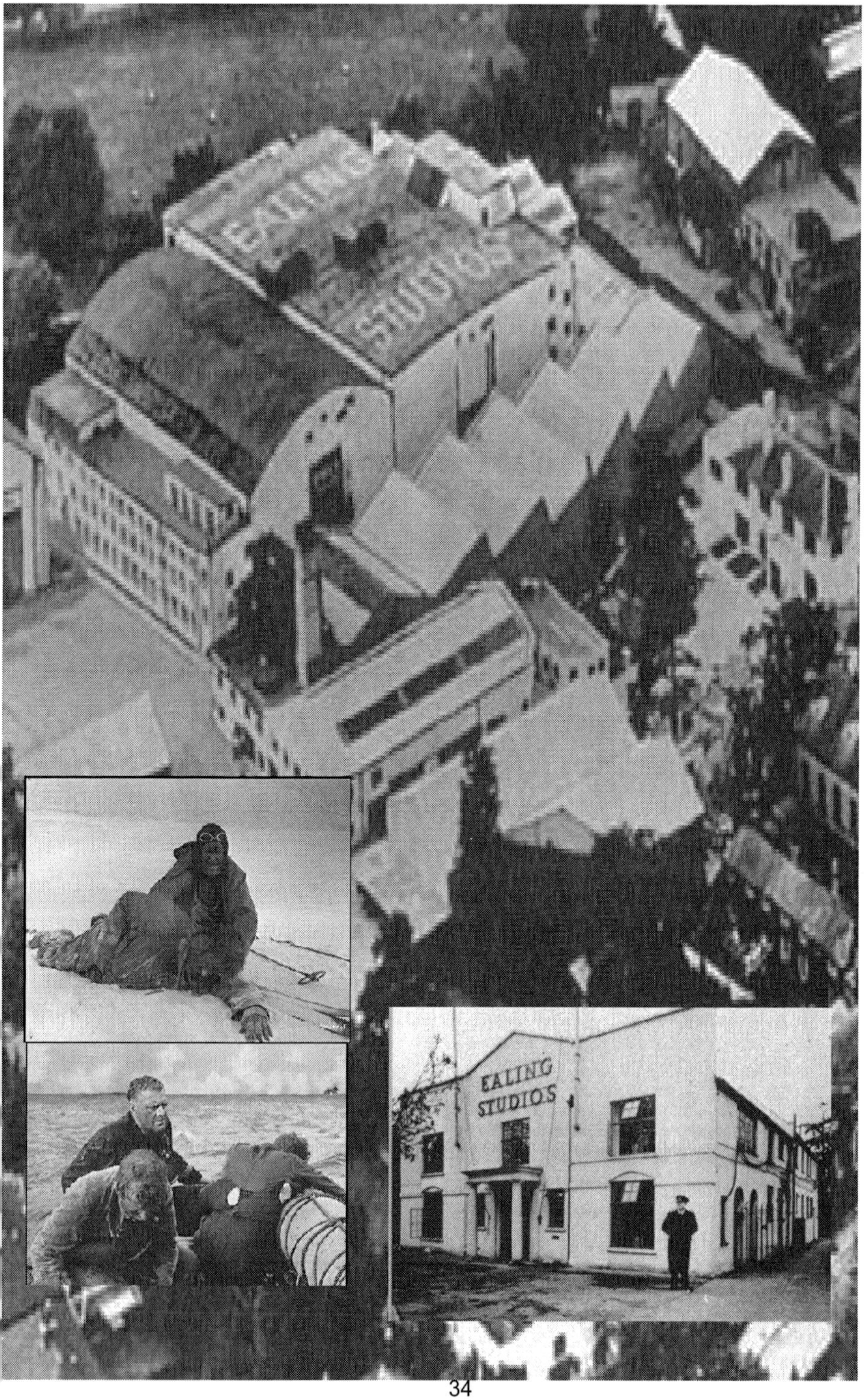
EALING
STUDIOS
EALING
STUDIOS

I arrived promptly at 9.30am for my first days work in any film studio. From the outside Ealing is small by studio standards. It doesn't look impressive but, as I passed through its doors for the first time I instantly felt I was entering a very special place. I was walking in the footsteps of giants. Michael Balcon had lead many geniuses this way. As I walked from what was once his office to the main sound stages, I wondered what young Alec Guinness had felt like when he had stepped the same way to splay all the main parts in KIND HEARTS AND CORONETS. One of the greatest film classics of all time. It had been shot in the studio I was about to enter.

As I walked on I passed Film Despatch and the Preview Theatres where rushes were screened each day. Alongside was a power house where huge generators ran day and night to provide all the power the studio required. It was opposite a sound stage where John Mills had starred in SCOTT OF THE ANTARCTIC - an early Technicolor feature about Scott's adventures in the Antarctic, which was filmed at Ealing. In those days colour films needed an enormous amount of light. Film stocks were not as sensitive as they are today. I remember Mills explaining how difficult it had been acting as if they were in sub zero temperatures, when in fact they were at Ealing studios, fully clad in arctic gear, and surrounded by ten kilowatt arc lamps which made their studio set as hot as a sauna.

The studio next door had been used for even bigger epics. It had a huge water tank which had been built into in the middle of the floor. It had seen service in a number of Ealing films. Jack Hawkins and Donald Sinden had spent several days in it pretending to be marooned on a life raft in the middle of the Atlantic. That film was THE CRUEL SEA. In my view one of the best British war films produced at that time. The tank shots were inter-cut with footage shot on real ships at sea and it was done so well no one ever suspected there were studio sets.

Involved. The Director of that film was Charles Frend who had been a Film Editor in Ealing's cutting rooms, which was where I was to start my career.

On my first day at Ealing I was told what I could expect to learn on my three year training course and how it would be conducted. I had been given an idea of its general scope but the details had not been discussed. When they were revealed it was encouraging news. Unlike many training courses, which are conducted in classrooms and at special training centres, we were to be trained "on the job". We would be attached individually to programme production teams and work alongside them for a month each time. In practice that meant we would work on children's programmes, then spend a month on one of the topical magazine programmes which went out at peak times. Attachments to light entertainment, sport and other departments would follow until we had worked on most of the main types of programme the BBC produced. We would be expected to acquire first hand practical experience of the many different skills required to make television programmes. We would be interviewed at regular intervals to see how we were getting on. Producers in charge of programmes we were attached to would be asked at end of each month of we were any good. At the end of the course, if we had proved the BBC had made the right choice in selecting us, we would be offered a job on the BBC's permanent staff. After being Trainee Assistants for three years we would have new job titles and be Editors, Cameramen, Sound Recordists or whatever, on a full salary with a secure job. From our first day training we would be paid as we learned. We did not get a fortune but my first pay was more than I had earned when I was working for Rank. I would probably have worked for nothing if I had been asked as I was enjoying it so much.

I had been lucky enough to join the BBC (British Broadcasting Corporation - not company as many often seem to think.) at the best possible time. The Corporation was an acknowledged world leader in international broadcasting, with a reputation to match. In two world wars BBC broadcasts had been beamed round the world and it had earned a well deserved reputation for accuracy and quality. Radio programmes transmitted from London had reached every corner of the earth. Television was new to everyone, in Britain and overseas. The BBC had stared to experiment with basic equipment in a small studio at Alexandra Palace in North London in 1938. Work stopped at the outbreak of the war but, when peace returned tests were resumed. As people began to think television might perhaps have some possibilities test transmissions started again. At that time a popular BBC radio programme (known as a wireless programme then!) would be heard by around five million people in the UK alone. Millions more tuned in overseas. Television pictures could only be received within a few miles of the north London transmitter. They were viewed in black and white on sets which had a screen size about twelve inches across and regularly broke down. By the time I started my television training scheme much progress had been made. The BBC had established the country's only television service which went on air for a few hours each day. Sound and picture quality were gradually improving but it still sometimes looked as if programmes were being seen through a snowstorm and transmissions regularly broke down. When that happened a caption would advise viewers that "normal services will be resumed as soon as possible". Soothing music would then be played while frantic efforts were made to sort out problems. The Corporation gradually acquired theatres and other premises which could be used for its television activities in various parts of London. One of those acquisitions was Ealing Studios where my training started in the cutting rooms.

When I first considered a film industry career the prospect of becoming a Producer or Director had appealed to me for all the wrong reasons. I associated it with glamour and prestige as many others have. When I eventually directed my first film I had worked professionally in the business for ten years. By then I knew why my initial thoughts were wrong. As my brief descriptions of location filming experiences at the start of this book have probably already shown you, glamour and prestige are not the first thought you have in mind when you are shooting in difficult conditions, have to remain on schedule and in budget and have a crews and cast who are depending on you. I could never have directed anything without the experience I had gained on location, in studios and above all the 5 years I spent working in cutting rooms. There you really learn what you need to make a film or a television programme work. You start with basic raw materials. Sounds and pictures which you have to assemble in the right order and then use them creatively to achieve the desired end result. Perhaps you want to scare people or make them laugh. Or maybe your goal is to make points clear or encourage the audiences who will see your finished work to do, or not do, something. If you do not have the right materials to work with, you will be unable to do what you want. You must know what shots to shoot and where to shoot them from, so they can be cut together without problems. Film crews can spot an inexperienced Director a mile off. If you are in charge of a production and don't know what you are doing they will soon find out. When they do you will lose their respect and, without that, you may face an uphill task.

If you have learned enough about their particular skills they will appreciate that you know what you are doing. Progress will be easier and the results should be good. You will not ask a Cameraman to shoot something in an impractical way or a Recordist to record sounds in impossible conditions. Together you will work out the best way of doing things.

My first day in a professional cutting room was spent working on a popular childrens' programme - *ANDY PANDY*, which had been shot on 35mm film. It seemed a strange film to be editing in a cutting room where they had cut such classics as THE *LADY KILLERS,* and *THE LAVENDER HILL MOB,* but you have to start somewhere and the BBC had obviously decided I should start at the top! As I had never been in a cutting room before, the Editor, in whose room I had been placed, introduced me to the equipment I would have to use and then explained my task for the day. He had edited feature films for years and was clearly bored with having to show a Trainee a very basic task but he knew what he was doing and his instructions were clear. "This is the programme they are showing tonight", he said handing me several cans of 35mm film. Your job is to join on the titles. I will show you how to do it and then it's up to you. "The titles are in there" he continued, indicating another can of film. "It's quite straightforward but you need to watch out. There are 2 sets of titles and they are not the same. One says "Andy Pandy is in his little house today. Let's go join him." " The other says he's in his bleedin' garden. So, check the label first! If you get the wrong ones we'll get lots of phone calls from pissed off kids." He turned and headed for the door before adding "When you have finished take it down to Telecine and then come and join me. You'll find me opposite reception, in the pub."

Later than afternoon, on the pub's television, we watched as childrens' television started. *ANDY PANDY* was the first programme to be shown. As it started to run I prayed that I had got the title the right way up and that the join I had made would not fall apart. Fortunately all went well and my new colleague bought the next pint. I had passed my first test. My career had begun!

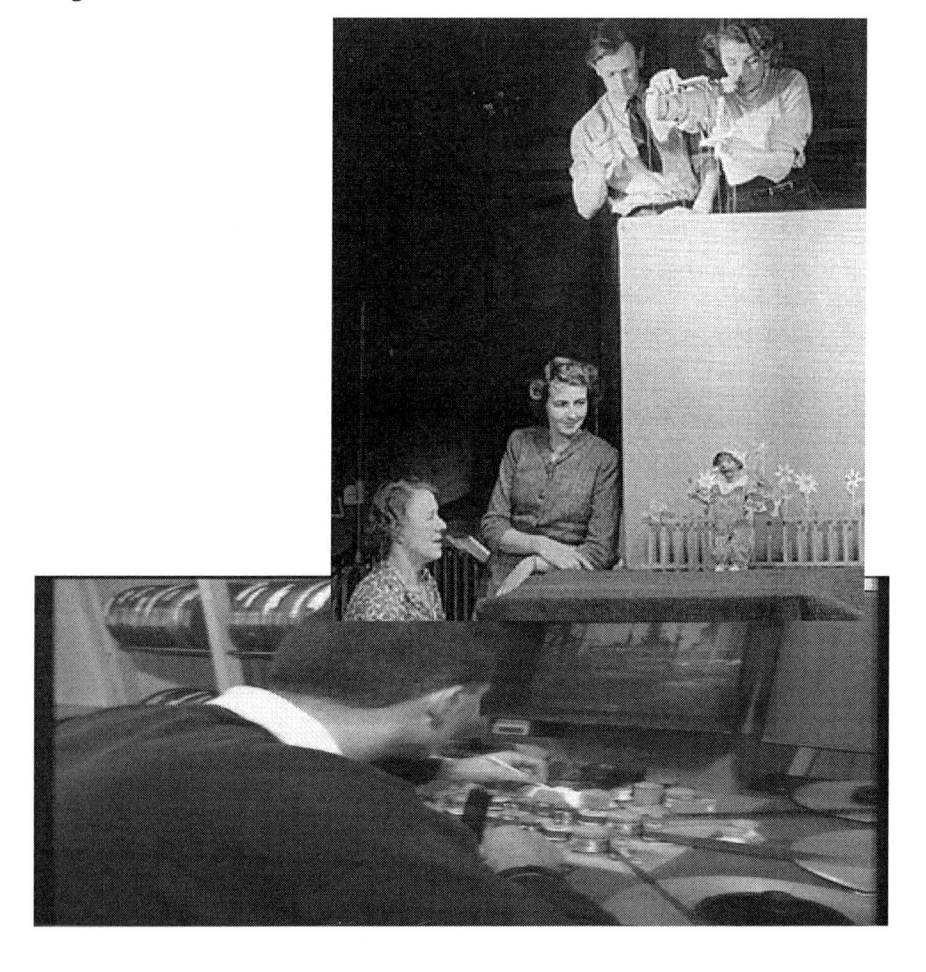

After such a momentous start, I wondered what task I would be given next. I didn't have to wait long to find out. The following day I was told I was being promoted - from *ANDY PANDY* to *THE FLOWERPOT MEN* - another programme which was popular with many kids. I only worked on it for for a few days but it was great fun. People who make programmes for children are a very special breed. They often have to work on tight budgets and achieve miracles but the fantasy worlds they create are full of magic, colour, light and joy. When I joined the BBC the most popular children's programmes were the ones I have already mentioned and *BLUE PETER*- a well established live studio romp which became a national institution. There was also *CAPTAIN PUGWASH*- a programme made with cardboard cut out characters by Gordon Murray - another great pioneer. As a child he had been fascinated by puppets. When he grew up he built a small puppet theatre to entertain his friends at home. He then acquired a clockwork 16mm Bolex film camera. It was not designed for professional use but Murray had a garage and he used it to build small scale sets and shoot films. The characters he created and the stories his films told were wonderfully inventive and he was encouraged to show them to a friend who happened to work for the BBC. The Corporation recognised his outstanding talents and his films were soon being appreciated by audiences far and wide. Murray went on to build a puppet television studio and produce films which were sold all all over the world. In the course of his work he created hundreds of memorable characters and told stories which appealed to children and adults alike. In 1980 he decided he had had enough and wanted to do something else. He burned all but one of the puppets and sets he had created and started making limited edition miniature books. Several years later, when he was planning to retire, he found a number of reels of film which he had forgotten. He gave them to be BBC. Now they have been digitally restored so some of his wonderful creations can be enjoyed by a new generation.

After meeting The Flowerpot Men I was told to join the people who were working in the cutting rooms next door. That proved to be a major advance because I found myself working with some of the most interesting and creative people I have ever met. They were all to become very famous figures. Two went on to senior management positions and all of them had an enormous impact on the future of television in the UK and overseas. When I first met him a young David Attenborough had just returned from a trip overseas. He was sitting in the canteen at Ealing with a number of colleagues. David, in addition to his many other talents, is a wonderful raconteur. I cannot recall what he was saying at that time but I know it was a very funny story and it involved a snake. Others round the table included Charles Lagus - a young cameraman who had been involved in filming the recent conquest of Everest. Working in sub zero conditions he had assisted another cameraman (Tom Stobart) to capture that historic moment. Alongside there were members of the production team who were working with David on his latest project - a series called *ZOO QUEST*. I was to be attached to them to see what went on.

After completing his National Service David had worked in publishing for a while. He then joined the BBC. He started at Alexandra Palace , joined the Talks Department and was taught basic interviewing techniques. He then tried to use them in a few early television programmes which were produced with very little money on obsolete equipment. It is important to remember that in the 1950s, when the events we were involved in were taking place, none of the equipment or modern facilities we rely on today existed. Mobile phones, video and most of the things we use to make programmes today were just pipe dreams. Shows went out "live". Audiences saw whet went on - mistakes and all. It was not until 1958 that the first electronic recordings were made. Until then pictures had to be photographed on photographic film. It then had to be processed by a film laboratory before it could be viewed.. Sound was recorded in another photographic process until about the same time when it started to be recorded magnetically.

It all took time and cost money and was much more harder work than it is today.

When David and I were working at Ealing Studio, his ZOO QUEST programme was a Talks Department production. In its early days "Experts" from London Zoo were invited to bring interesting animals into a studio where they could be televised while the Experts were interviewed. Anyone who lived near enough to a transmitter to receive a signal would then be able to watch. Audiences loved the shows because they introduced hem to things they might otherwise never see. David wrote the scripts and conducted the interviews and the series began to attract attention. The disadvantages of live television were readily apparent. The few cameras which were available were large and cumbersome. They had to be connected to a control room by lots of cables and they needed a lot of light to see anything at all. David wanted to use film for the animals and live television just for the interviews but the BBC were not keen. At that time they would only use 35mm film and that cost money. Inspired by the people who had filmed the conquest of Everest David suggested they should shoot on 16mm film. It was cheaper and more transportable. The BBC film department dismissed the idea out of hand. Like most other professional film makers then, they described 16mm as "bootlaces" or "spaghetti" and felt it was only suitable for amateur use. The battle continued for months but eventually David won. A short time after that "spaghetti" became television's staple diet For the first but certainly not the last time, David Attenborough had lead the way.

ZOO QUEST broke new ground and forced those who were set in their ways to consider new ideas and try innovative equipment and techniques. Throughout his career Attenborough encouraged innovation and was never afraid of venturing into the unknown. His programmes set new standards which other Producers wanted to emulate. When the BBC agreed to let him use a small film camera and then to shoot overseas he won two a major victories. Zoo keepers no longer had to be asked to bring their animals to him. He could now travel to distant places and find animals people had probably never seen or even heard of. They could be shown in their natural environments and could then be brought back to zoos where their needs would be properly understood. Experts could then be invited to a studio to hold their discussions. It was an entirely new concept and a tremendous success.

The ZOO QUEST team went on to visit many countries which few people then would have been able to explore. They went to Guyana, New Guinea, Paraguay and South America .Before modern jet aircraft and established shipping routes, it took time, money and above all effort to get anywhere which was off the beaten track. At Cambridge David had studied natural science so he was the ideal man to lead such expeditions. He knew what to look for and where it was. Before the modern age of mass air travel and well established shipping routes, getting anywhere off the beaten track was extremely difficult to organize. If you eventually managed to get where you wanted to be, you needed an explorer's mentality and stamina to achieve your objectives. David and Charles Lagus faced lots of problems they had to to contend with. They had a portable camera but it could only run continuously for about a minute They shot on black and white film. Colour film was then just a distant myth. The film stock they used needed a lot of light to get any exposure at all and, in the tropical forests where they wanted to film, there was often so little light it was hard to get around. They did not have any long focus lenses and zoom lenses did not exist. So they had to get very close to everything they filmed.

Their camera only shot on silent film. Any sounds had to to be recorded by David using a separate battery powered portable tape recorder. It ran at one speed. The camera at another and there as no way of synchronising the two, so interviewing someone in vision was out of the question. To add sound at all miracles had to be achieved later in the cutting rooms. It was uphill work but miracles were achieved almost every day. Today doing what David and his team achieved then would be so much easier, but now it would be too late. Much of what they saw then has has been destroyed in the name of progress.

After years spent making a number of classic television series, which won numerous awards and were shown around the world, David allowed himself to be persuaded to take a senior management job as Controller of what was then as new national network - BBC 2. He spent four years trying to ensure the network showed high quality programmes and was heading for the right goals. He then returned to full time production.

When my brief attachment to ZOO QUEST came to and end I was moved to another talks department programme which was also headed by a man who was to become one of the leading figures in the British television.

When I first met Huw Wheldon he was a Presenter, a Producer and a senior BBC Executive. He was also in charge of the corporation's flagship television arts programme. It was called *MONITOR. It* was a weekly magazine programme which consisted of inserts shot on film and studio scenes, which usually meant interviews, with people whose artistic achievements were in the news. Arts programmes are not popular with television companies because they do not attract mass audiences like *CORONATION STREET* and *EAST ENDERS*. They only appeal to the limited number of people who have an interest in the arts. *MONITOR* set out to broaden that scope. For years it was the only television arts programme but, when commercial television started, London Weekend Television introduced *AQUARIUS* and T*HE SOUTH BANK*

SHOW. Two excellent arts programme which made Melvyn Bragg a sought after television personality almost overnight. They did very well but MONITOR had a secret weapon - Huw Wheldon - and when I joined the production team in the course of my training. I was able to watch him at work.

On first acquaintance I wondered how on earth he had managed to do so well. He had a slightly hesitant way of speaking and peered at you through bushy eyebrows with his head tending to tilt from side to side. His whole approach was rather casual but he did not miss a trick. As I watched him at work I soon saw why he had achieved so much in a very short time.

On the day we first met he was about to interview a man who had come to Ealing to show him a film. After being pursued for weeks Huw had finally caved in and and agreed to watch the film. As I was with him at that time he asked I would like to watch it with him. We went into one of Ealing's preview theatres with the youngish man whose film it was. He was looked "artistic". I later learned that after spending time in the merchant navy and then in the RAF he had become a ballet dancer. I had noticed that he wore rather strange shoes with very long laces which were not tied up so they trailed behind him. His name was Ken Russell.

As a projectionist prepared to run the film, it's Producer mentioned that he had made it to try and capture the spirit of the place where he as living. That is why he had called it *"A HOUSE IN BAYSWATER"*. He then added that he hoped the film would speak for itself.

The film we then saw had been produced on a shoestring budget with basic equipment, but when it ended, for several minutes nobody spoke. We were aware that just seen a masterpiece. It was one of the most interesting films I had seen up to then and one I still recall with great pleasure to this day. By the end of that day our visiting film maker had been offered a job. He had explained that he had a number of ideas for films which he had always wanted to make and Huw suggested he should make them for *MONITOR*. For the next six weeks I worked alongside and watched as the first of those films began to take shape.

Ken had a number of passions in life. Today he is largely remembered for the feature films he made but his early television work was just as striking and produced in a very simple way. One of his abiding passions was music. Shortly after his arrival a gramaphone was installed in our cutting room at Ealing. The BBC has one of the best collections of records in the world and, as a member of staff working on programmes we only had to pick up an internal phone and call the gramaphone library to find almost anything any record lover could ever want. The staff were knowledgeable and interested in their work and Ken lost no time in enlisting their support.

Our cutting room was filled with music all day long as Ken started to explore some of his ideas. After tactfully leaving him alone for a week Huw then asked if there were any particular ideas which Ken would like to follow up. His answer surprised us all. He said he would like to make a film about the Russian composer Sergi Prokofiev.

It seemed an odd subject to choose for an English television programme and there were a few other problems, as Huw was quick to point out. Prokofiev was dead. He had died on same day as Stalin eight years ago. He had spent most of his life in Russia and at that time England and Russia were not the best of friends. As far as we knew, there was no existing film footage of Prokofiev at all. But Ken wasn't worried. He had been captivated by the composer's music. As I was the youngest member of the production team, he turned to me and asked what I thought. I explained that I loved the records he had played, but my only experience of music had been gained at school, where I had played the organ for morning service in our school chapel. As I could not read music and played by ear, we had the same three hymns rather a lot. With the courage and vision no one in today's BBC would ever understand, Huw told him to go ahead and see what he could do.

If you want to know what foresight and vision are all about, ask yourself what you would have done at that point. Ken had been given six weeks to produce a film about a man who was dead and on whom no life time footage was known to exist. There was as yet no script and, apart from recordings of his music nothing else at all to make our film with.

Ken listed the points in the composer's life that he wanted to explore. What had inspired his music and how had it been received when it was performed. What images did it conjure up and what had the Composer wanted it to portray and achieve? Gradually a theme emerged and that theme was then broken down into subjects we would have to illustrate. Ken wanted to use an actor to appear as the Composer but Huw hated the idea and refused to support it. There were heated arguments but no agreement could be reached. Huw passionately believed that documentaries should only include actual footage of the subjects they portrayed.

People reflected in lakes, or giving a similarly vague impression elsewhere, would also be acceptable but any attempt to impersonate the Composer in full view of the camera would not be considered. As I think you will agree, the future for Ken was not looking bright.

The resulting film was a masterpiece of imagination and technique. Library footage of the 1917 Russian revolution and scenes from old Russian feature films was obtained from every possible source. We viewed hundreds of films showing every aspect of Russian life at the time when Prokofiev had been alive. Gradually, in Ken's fertile mind our film began to take shape. Additional footage was staged and shot, without breaking Wheldon's rules. In the skilled hands of one one of the best Cameramen in the business (Ken Higgins) and an equally experienced and talented film Editor (Alan Tyrer) a masterpiece began to emerged. I learned a lot working on that programme. It was shot and edited on 35mm film as most of the library film we acquired has been in that format. I learned how film can be enlarged, reduced, copied and improved to meet the needs of today. A basic knowledge of how film laboratories work was needed too. As there was no sound on any of the library footage we had to create every sound the audience would hear.
That meant recording and mixing thousands of different sounds and making them work with our edited pictures. From the the camera team I learned how to use lights creatively and control focus so we could show audiences what we wanted them to see. I watched as they made two people sitting in an empty London theatre look as if they were in a Moscow opera house, in the midst of an enthusiastic crowd. It's amazing what you can achieve with a few lights and mirrors if you know what to do!

Ken went on to greater things. His passion for music was further developed when in 1962 he made the definitive film on the life of Sir Edward Elgar - another Composer he admired. That film won a number of awards and established Russell as one of England's most talented up and coming Directors.

From *MONITOR* he moved from the BBC to the world of feature films. It was an entirely different working environment. In the BBC, If they they wanted to go off and shoot a particular scene on a day when the weather happened to be right for what they wanted to achieve, they just went off and did it. In the world of feature films that could not be done. With fully unionised crews, internal political battles and temperamental casts he was out of his depth. His early feature films were not a great success but he went on to make a number of classics. Alas today he is not with us any more. He died of cancer in 1986 at the age of 84

Huw Wheldon stayed with the BBC. He became Head of Documentaries and then Controller of BBC 1. In 1968 he was made Managing Director of BBC Television. He was knighted in 1976. When he died of cancer in 1986 his ashes were spread anonymously in the Royal Botanic Gardens at Kew, where he had served as a Trustee for many years. It was a place he had always loved, and the studios where he had achieved so much were just minutes away.

From *MONITOR* I moved from the film studios at Ealing to work on live television programmes in some of the studios and other premises the BBC was using at that time. Everyone was waiting for a new Television Centre to be built. The site of the old White City Stadium had been cleared and plans for a new purpose built building which would house all the different departments needed to produce television programmes under one roof had been drawn up and approved. While construction was underway programmes had to be made in a number of buildings which the BBC had leased. The biggest and most used was the old Gaumont British film studio in Lime Grove Shepherd's Bush. Other key buildings used at that time included the smaller Riverside studio in Hammersmith and what had been the Shepherds Bush Empire theatre. There cameras and a control room had been installed and it was now known as The Television Theatre. It was there that popular light entertainment programmes were staged.

THE BLACK AND WHITE MINSTREL SHOW, produced by George Inns and starring the George Mitchell Minstrels was transmitted from the Television Theatre for several years. The theatre was also home to a number of shows aimed at families. One of the most popular, which took place every week, was presented by a celebrity who usually smoked a cigar and always arrived in a Rolls Royce. We thought he was a bit odd but odd celebrities were nothing new, so we did not take much notice. Several years later we were to learn how odd he was. His name was Jimmy Savile!

In my time at Ealing I had been able to learn more in a few months, that I would probably do today in just as many years. I was lucky enough to be in the right place at the right time. Television was new and expanding fast. I was was not shut away in classrooms being lectured by people who had probably forgotten how to do what they had once done or never done much in the first place. That is what can happen today, on what are often temptingly described as "multi media courses". Students do not get paid while they are learning and at the end of their studies many end with a worthless degree or some other piece of paper which potential employers will quickly dismiss. There are some very good universities and film schools but they are few and far between. Unfortunately there are also many where the syllabus is too diverse.

An in depth knowledge of film history is nice to have but it may not be worth spending twelve months acquiring. If you are looking for a job making films today you should have more pressing concerns.

You need to know how to write and read scripts; how to use cameras of various types and what different microphones can do with sound. If you are working in television or making films, you must understand what editing is all about Only then will you be able to ensure you have the right raw materials to work with and can use them in the most effective way. Multi media is a very vague term. It can cover anything from using a computer to do a mundane job to producing original and ground breaking special effects. So, if you are planning to study before you start your career, do some research before you sign up. Another potential problem it pays to watch out for is the equipment you will be expected to use. Is it reasonably up to date or are you being taught on machines or with software which is no longer in everyday use. Who will your fellow students be? That too is worth some thought. Unfortunately there are some establishments where they will sign up anyone who can pay their fees. I have seen courses where most of the students are from overseas. They are there because their governments have given them a grant. That does not necessarily mean they are interested in film or able to understand the language in which the skills the are there to acquire are being taught.

The studios at Lime Grove Shepherd's Bush, in the London borough of Hammersmith and Fulham, first opened in 1915. They were built for Gaumont (later Gaumont British) and the original structure was basically a wooden shell built to support a glass roof above open sets so filming could be done in daylight. In the 1930s the original structure was replaced by a much sturdier multi storey building. In 1934 a young Alfred Hitchcock made one of his first films there. It was *THE MAN WHO KNEW TOO MUCH,* starring a young Peter Lorre who, like Hitchcock Himself. was just starting his career.

The BBC bought the studio in 1949 intending to use it as a stop gap while their new Television Centre was being built. When I arrived,towards the end of the 1950s, it was being used as the main base for a topical programmes unit. That was where I was to continue my training and it was generally considered a good place to be. When I worked there it was home to many of the nation's top television programmes. *PANORAMA, GRANDSTAND* (which became *SPORTSVIEW,* and *TONIGHT* all came from there. *TONIGHT,* attracted huge audiences as it went out "live" every weekday at 6pm, when people were getting home from work.

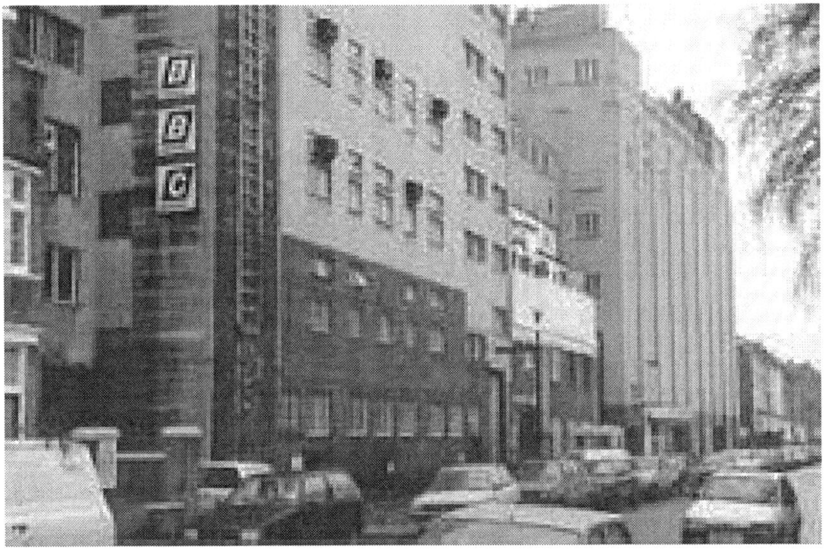
B
B
C

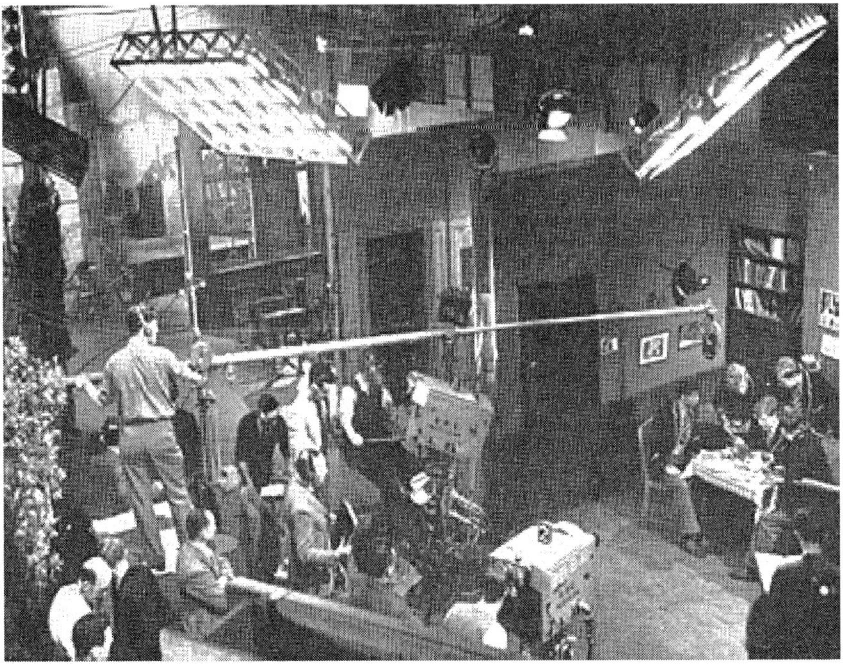

Each programme ran for half an hour and *TONIGHT* proved so popular that it remained a key element in BBC programming until 1965. As video recordings did not exist everything we transmitted was shot on film in advance or or transmitted live from studio 4 at Lime Grove so getting programmes on air was quite a job. Fortunately it was in the hands of a superb production team. On screen and off camera those involved had been chosen because they knew what to do and would not panic if things went wrong, as they did almost every night.

The programmes were presented (or"anchored",as we used to say,by Cliff Michelmore. He had started his career in radio presenting a popular radio programme - *FAMILY FAVOURITES* - so live broadcasting was not new to him. Television broadcasting was, as it was to most of us. We were living in an age where formal Presenters and Newsreaders with stiff collars and neatly pressed suits had become the norm. Cliff was the first to become "one of us". He always seemed to be totally relaxed and he spoke to viewers as if they were neighbours or friends. They loved him because he was totally down to earth.

When films broke down as they were being shown, Cliff always seemed to be in command. A phone on his desk would ring. Whoever was directing the show that day would tell him we were going to miss out a couple of items, and go on to something which was scheduled to come much later in the programme. While, off stage, we were frantically trying to repair the film Cliff had to forget he was being watched by several million viewers and dream up a link which would enable him to move from the film about coal mining, which our audience had been watching, to a story we had shot in Canada a few days before. He did it so well audiences adored him, as did we who had to sort out the mess !

Working on *TONIGHT* I was surrounded by talent. The pace was hectic but the people who put the programme together always found time to explain what they were doing. In a surprisingly short time I was being treated as one of the team. I learned how to synchronise rushes and how stories shot on film were processed. I began to acquire the many different skills which are needed to turn reels on unedited film into a coherent story which can be shown on air. I sat alongside as hand written notes made on location were turned into scripts which could be recorded in a dubbing theatre minutes before transmission. I saw how nervous people waiting to be interviewed could be put at ease. While they relaxed, their interrogators showed me how they prepared their questions. If their wording was inept they might not get the answers they required and could end up with minutes of " yes" and "no.

One of my best tutors who, in the months I worked with him taught me everything anyone could ever want to know about television reporting had started his his career in the army film unit. He had joined *TONIGHT* before me and had quickly established himself as a key part of the programme and a popular national figure. His career was to to last for nearly sixty years and take him round the word numerous times. His name was Alan Whicker.

I first met Alan in the cutting rooms on the 7th floor at Lime Grove early one morning. He had just got back from a trip to Canada where he had shot a number of stories which would be used in the programme in the coming weeks. As always, he was immaculately dressed in a blue blazer, well pressed trousers and a tasteful tie. I was introduced to him as I was the youngest and newest member of the the production team. He could not have been more friendly or helpful if I had been a member of the Royal Family. An innately quiet and modest man with a great sense of humour, he had arrived early to work on one of the stories he had shot in Canada. Today we would probably Describe it as a Jurassic Park story.

Dinosaurs were not then everyday news but in Alberta Canada, as a tourist attraction, they had built a park which in many ways anticipated the settings which would prominently feature in those later films. Whicker and a *TONIGHT* film crew had paid them a visit and they had shot a witty and informative report. The film had been flown back from Canada and processed overnight at a film laboratory in north London. Sound, which had been recorded on location quarter inch tapes, had been re-recorded ("transferred" was the term we normally used) to perforated magnetic film so it could be synchronised and edited. Production teams today have a much easier job. They can record sounds and pictures together electronically, in full colour, on a camera or computer. By pressing a key they can see what they have shot and instantly send it anywhere in the world. In television in the 1950 and 60s we transmitted live programmes every night but scenes which needed to be shot on location always had to be filmed. That meant that the deadlines we had to meet could became quite a challenge.

Like all Reporters returning from location filming, Alan wanted to see what had been shot. Before that could happen the sound and picture rushes had to be synchronised so they could be viewed in one of Lime Grove's preview theatres or on an editing machine. As the most junior member the team, that was one of my jobs so I started to get on with it.

When you are handling rushes on a programme which is going on air that day, you cannot hang around. You have got to know what you are doing. Deadlines won't wait. To help me I had information sheets (known simply as "dope sheets), prepared by the Cameraman and sound Recordist who shot and recorded the film which now lay in a dozen cans in front of me. If they were good, and most BBC crews were, the sheets would provide all the help I needed to get the job done. They would list each scene and take and tell me if it was shot with sound or "mute".

If it was "mute" the Sound man might have recorded extra unsynchronised sounds which could be added in dubbing and that might be found later on the roll. If he was good, everything would be noted on his sheets. If the crew was having an off day or the story had been shot by a crew who did not care, vital information might not be there. Then every scene would have to be checked visually and aurally, slate by slate and that would take time.

It was always helpful if any of the Reporters or Directors involved were around when rushes were being prepared but, as the work was often done at unsociable hours, they were often still in bed or in the pub. What to do then was another of the many lessons I learned on my training course. On the morning I first met Alan Whicker, everything seemed to be in order and I stared work. As I wound through the reels of film, synchronising sound and picture scene by scene and slate by slate, Whicker opened a briefcase and took out some notes. He had his own copies of the camera and sound sheets. He had also made his own notes which he would use later when he had to write and record a commentary for scenes which had been shot without any sound at all. The story we were editing had been shot on a whistle stop tour of Canada. In a few days they had to film a number of reports at locations which were sometimes difficult to reach. Time was short and everyone was working under pressure.

In television that is quite normal but it can cause problems. Here it did not. Alan's notes were all handwritten and neatly filed. In seconds he could find anything he required and, when you are editing a programme which is going to be shown on national television in a few hours time, that kind of efficiency is priceless. As I got on with my work, Alan read through his notes. When I came to a scene which did not have a slate he recalled that a camera battery had gone flat when it was being shot. It had been retaken later. I checked the sheets and there it was, at the start of the next roll. - Scene 27 Take 2. It is so much easier when you know what you are looking for.

FROM SHOOT TO SCREEN BEFORE VIDEO

Like many everyday programmes work had actually started the day before. Then the production team had held a preliminary meeting to consider a number of stories which might perhaps be included in the programme we were now working on. An outline running order was then drawn up. Everyone knew that in the next 24 hours it would be changed many times and the programme that would eventually be transmitted might end up with none of the items listed being used at all. It was just a start and a goal to aim for. Overnight a small team would continue to work on the outline and add any new stories which might come in. That proved to be just as well because at 2am a news story broke which was to affect us all.

It was at that early hour that news agencies first reported that a light aircraft had signalled it was in trouble just west of Dover. An SOS message had been received from an aircraft which appeared to have crashed in the sea.

While emergency services along the south coast were alerted, at Lime Grove the duty F.O.M (Film Operations Manager) got a call from the overnight team working on *TONIGHT*. They needed a film crew to go immediately to Manston airport in Kent where they were arranging for a light aircraft suitable for filming to be prepared.

While that was being done the BBC's Aviation Correspondent (Reginald Turnill) was woken up in bed and told what had apparently been happening of the coast near Dover. He was told that a car would be arriving in fifteen minutes to take him to Manston where a crew would be waiting. Turnill was a very experienced reporter. He was used to being called on at short notice and took it all in his stride.

By nine o clock that morning, at Lime Grove Alan , I and the staff in the cutting room were getting on well with what we had to do. In the cutting room next door another team was working on another story to be screened that night. It was a report on the problems of the fishing industry in Scotland. It had been filmed by Another Reporter on the *TONIGHT* team - Fyffe Robertson- an excellent Reporter and a true Scot. I saw his report again in 2014. It was on *YOU TUBE*, and it brought back a lot of memories. I was surprised how good it looked. Like most old stories it had been shot in black and white but the camera work was superb. Every shot was nicely framed and expertly shot. Fyffe had captured the spirit of the story brilliantly. The difficulties Fishermen were starting to face then were very like those their successors complain about today, Fyffe had got them to talk about their problems in a way few Reporters would be able to achieve and the results were entrancing. The fish we saw were far bigger than anything anyone would ever catch today and the story was as interesting to watch as it was when it was made.

As Fyffe's fishing story and our Jurassic report were beginning to take shape, in offices down below the Director responsible for today's programme was making a final list of the subjects he hoped he would be able to include.

The two film stories were both on the list as they ere almost certain to be finished in time, though on a programme with such close deadlines as ours nothing could ever be completely guaranteed. A technical hitch in a dubbing theatre minutes before transmission could cause chaos even when the programme was on air.

On many occasions I worked on shows where part two was still being dubbed while part one was on the air. If you were properly prepared you could take it on your stride and took a pride in getting things right. The filmed stories would together run for eighteen minutes. To fill the rest of the programme's allotted time two more items were going to be needed.

On *TONIGHT* we had two resident Musicians - Robin Hall and Jimmy McGregor - who could be relied on to write and perform topical songs at the drop of a hat. Another popular singer- Cy Grant - was also on call. Their appearances were not always noted on the running order. If something went wrong they could be called on to perform at any minute. It happened quite a lot. Films would break down or jam. Studio cameras, which were enormous by today's standards, would overheat and their pictures would become blurred. Then a Floor Manager would be told to get Robin and Jimmy ready to perform. They would immediately move to a part oft the studio where lights were permanently rigged in case they needed to appear. While Cliff told viewers we had a slight technical problem, Robin and Jimmy would pick up their instruments. Lights above them would come on and the Floor Manager would raise an arm ready to drop it when, on the headphones he wore he heard the Director stay "Stand by Robin and Jimmy, and cue!"

At Manson as dawn broke Reg Turnill and a bleary eyed film crew, climbed into a small Cessna aircraft which the Film Operations Manager had managed to acquire. He had managed to persuade the Pilot to open a door in the side of the plane and pin it back so a Cameraman, suitably restrained by a harness, could get a clear view of what was taking place down below. That of course meant that the noise inside the plane would be horrendous. It would be very cold too but it should make it easier to get really good shots. At dawn the the aircraft took off and headed for Dover.

While it was on route, at Lime Grove the Producers were putting together their daily jigsaw puzzle. They needed one more item to complete he programme for the day. They decided to fill it by looking at a new book which was about to be published. It had been written by a man who had been a spitfire pilot in the second world war. In his book he recalled some of his experiences.

Researchers had contacted the Publishers and found out that the Author lived in Buckingham - near enough to be collected by car and brought to Lime Grove. As he was pondering which shirt to wear, at Lime Grove Designers working on a set for the programme were looking at the area where his interview would take place. The TONIGHT studio was not very big. By today's standards it would be regarded as minute but it served its purpose and every inch was used. The Director had said that he did not want a boring office type interview, with the Author sitting in a chair. Could the Designers make it look as if he was being interviewed on an airfield or at his Spitfire base? They said they thought they could and discussions were adjourned so they could see what they could do.

Above the English channel, in a very cold plane, Reg Turnill and his camera team had spotted a lifeboat working down below. On their first run past they managed to get a couple of shots but the Cameraman was not happy. The wing of their aircraft had got in the way at a critical point. He asked if the pilot could go round again.

At Lime Grove Fyffe Robertson's fishing report was finished and ready to roll. Alan Whicker's Jurassic Park story was almost in one piece but the final soundtrack still had to be recorded and dubbed.

Off the coast near Dover, on its third attempt attempt, a lifeboat had located some wreckage. Above them a camera had filmed them at work. It had a long fixed focus lens. Zoom lenses did not exist then. Shooting from a light aircraft buffeted by winds, with a long focus lens, and trying to hold it steady is an almost impossible task. The Cameraman asked if they could go round again. As the aircraft was repositioned the cameraman selected a wide angle lens. He knew that if he could use that the effects of the movement of the plane would be less obvious but to get a close enough shot they would need to fly much lower. Could that be done? The Pilot nodded his assent and the plane dropped down. This time everything fell into place at just the right time and the Cameraman was able to get the shot he felt he had needed. The aircraft turned and headed for home.

At Lime Grove set Designers had contacted The Imperial War Museum. They had been able to provide library shorts of spitfires in the air and still photographs of others parked on the ground. The *TONIGHT* Director thought he could use the flying shots as an introduction and then back project one of the stills on a large screen in front of which the author who was to be interviewed could be asked to sit. With a bit of subtle lighting he could then be made to look as if he was on a airfield.

By lunch time the likely shape the day's programme was at last becoming clear. After a quick snack in the canteen or the BBC club it as back to work with three and a half hours before our live transmission,

As the studio was prepared to set and light, at three o'clock the Director assessed what remained to be done. He might have film of a crashed aircraft being found in the Channel. That had just arrived from Manston at Finsbury Park in north London where it would be processed.

 If it was ready I time it would be brought to Lime Grove by a motorcycle Despatch Rider. If there was enough time, it would then be edited and put straight on air. In case that did not happen

Reg Turnill was somewhere between Manston and Lime Grove in another car. If the film was ready in time he could be interviewed and describe what he had seen as it was shown on air. If it did not make the deadline he would, be interviewed on his own against a plain blue background.

At 3pm, somewhere in Buckinghamshire the Author of a book, who had never been on television in his life, was on route to Lime Grove. There a projector was being lined up to show a life sized picture of two spitfires on a back projection screen. Fyffe Robertson's fisherman film was finished and ready to project.

In the cutting room where Alan Whicker and I were working, he was using a portable typewriter to complete a script he would read in a dubbing theatre three floors below in twenty minutes time .He read his words out loud, to make sure they would fit in the screen time available for each and every shot. By 5.30pm everything seemed ready and in the studio a rehearsal was underway.

There were still a few problems which had to be sorted out. An overhead lamp shone not on the Author, as had been intended, but on the back projection screen obliterating the parked aircraft scene it was supposed to project. That had to be corrected. The Author was sitting in a chair which creaked every time he moved and that needed to be replaced as the minutes ticked by.

With thirty minutes to go, Fyffe's film was in Telecine, laced up and and ready to run. Reg Turnill's film had arrived and was being edited on the 7th floor. Reg himself came in a few minutes ago and a pretty girl from makeup was doing her best to disguise the results of a very hard day.
Alan and I were dubbing a final mix soundtrack for his Jurassic Park film which was due to be shown in a 15 minutes.

If all went well we should just make it in time. If equipment broke down or someone missed a cue, we would have to go back to the top and record the whole reel again. If that happened we would miss our allocated slot and the running order would have to be changed while we were live on air with millions of people watching. With minutes to go we finished recording and raced up three flights of stairs to give the film to the Telecine Operator who would project it on transmission. As I handed it over I could hear the Director on talk back from his control room three floors below." Stand by Telecine." They laced up the film and finished just as we heard the Director's voice again. " Run Telecine!" We had made it on time!

TONIGHT went out live on five nights each week. At weekends at the time I was there, Lime Grove home to a number of other top programmes. DIXON OF DOCK GREEN was staged there. Eric Sykes, Hattie Jacques, Jimmy Edwards and many other big television stars were based there. Sykes not only starred in his shows. He also wrote the scripts. He had started writing radio shows including the very popular EDUCATING ARCHIE, in which many who were to become top international stars started their careers. He was being paid fifty guineas a script. His office was not in the studio itself. It was above a greengrocer's shop in the Shepherds Bush Road, which ran across the top of Lime Grove. He was a pleasant, modest and very talented man and his office soon became a Writers workshop. He was joined by Frankie Howerd, Spike Milligan and other budding talents. Their operations gradually expanded and they moved to prestigious premises elsewhere and eventually became Greater London Scripts. Shortly before his death in 2012, Sykes wrote a wonderful autobiography which he recalled those early days and his weekly television shows which were simply called SYKES AND A......

Towards the end of my time on TONIGHT I was asked if I would like to work one weekend on a pilot programme for a show they were going to try out Nobody seemed to think it would work but I thought it sounded interesting and agreed to get involved. It was to be a pilot programme for a science fiction programme and it would be recorded for archive purposes on film, as if it was being transmitted live.It would feature an actor who had just made CARRY ON SERGEANT at Pinewood Studio. His name was William Hartnell and he was to be the first DOCTOR WHO. Hartnell was a good, experienced actor. He had appeared in a number of feature films but television was relatively new to him. In our Lime Grove studio he seemed to be rather bewildered. He was used to appearing in feature films where scenes are shot one at a time with a single camera. There is plenty of time between each shot for actors to study their lines, while cameras are repositioned and sets lit. In a television studio production proceeds at a very different pace. The action is often filmed from beginning to end in one continuous take. As it proceeds a number of cameras around the set simultaneously shoot different shots from different angles. In a control gallery the Director and his team can instantly cut from one camera to another. There are no pauses between shots. Hartnell was obviously not prepared for that and at times had difficulty remembering his script. To make life easier for him, lines and cues were written on boards which were held just out If shot. If he had a problem he only had to casually glance at a board to pick up the theme. Eventually the recording ended and we knew the show was safely "in the can". No one thought it would ever ben seen by the public. The film was processed overnight, ready for me to edit the following day. In view of the acclaim that has been accorded to *DOCTOR WHO* in recent years perhaps it's just as well that someone decided to record that rather important test.

In 2012 the first two complete series of *DR WHO,* which featured William Hartnell and then Patrick Troughton, were digitally restored. Using equipment which was not available when the shows were made, the definition of the original archive recordings was considerably enhanced. Test have also been carried out on colouring some episodes using modern computers but so far the results have not been released.

Videotape first came to Britain in the 1960s. An American firm - Ampex - made the first machines that produced professional results. Before that at Lime Grove the BBC had secretly been trying to perfect their own system. I saw a prototype when I was there. The Engineers called it Vera. That stood for Vision Electronic Recording Apparatus. It was vast and it ran at a frightening speed. Twenty inch reels of magnetic tape passed over static magnetic recording and playback heads at a a speed of over five metres a second! The maximum recording time was about fifteen minutes and the apparatus took up a whole room. When the American Ampex system was launched Vera was quietly forgotten hut the BBC's effort was given one public showing. It was briefly demonstrated on the next programme I was to join - *PANORAMA*.

Working on *PANORAMA* was considered something of a coup. It was the most prestigious current affairs programme on television. It is still good today but then it really had no rivals. Commercial television did not get underway until 1955. *PANORAMA* went out once a week and it was hosted by a man who had already become a legend - Richard Dimbleby.

He started his career as a journalist working for the Richmond and Twickenham Times, which his family owned. From there he went to the Daily Echo in Southampton - a excellent newspaper then as as it still is today. Hr joined the BBC as a radio Reporter in 1936 and found himself on the Normandy beaches reporting from the front line on D day.

As the war progressed he flew as as Observer with RAF Bomber Command reporting raids on Berlin. As the war neared its end he was one of the first troops to arrive at Belsen. Surrounded by the dead and dying he wrote a report which was among the first to reveal to the world the horrors of that German concentration camp. It was an experience which haunted him for years.

At the BBC he became something of an icon. His wartime reports had been broadcast around the world so he was already an international figure. With him at the helm PANORAMA commanded respect and quickly established itself as the programme everyone with ambitions wanted to be on. Cabinet Ministers and even Prime Ministers talked to PANORAMA while lesser mortals were politely ignored.

Of course not everyone who sought to come on the programme was invited to appear. There were a number of well known personalities whose well publicised antics had too often attracted the interest of the press. One of those was Britain's Foreign Secretary at the time who had been carried out of several official functions in a legless state. When I was on the programme I hoped he would appear but alas he never did. I had to rely on the accounts of those who has seen him in action to find out what I had missed. Years later another excellent Journalist - Jeremy Paxman neatly summarised an event I had often heard described.

In Peru our Foreign Secretary had attended an official dinner in full formal dress - medals and all. There he was seen swaying across the room towards a purple apparition. When he reached his destination he asked the lovely lady if she would like to dance. " No" she replied, for three reasons. Firstly I don't dance with drunks. Secondly they are playing the Peruvian National Anthem and you should be standing to attention, and thirdly I am the Cardinal Archbishop of Lima."

PANORAMA was the BBC's flagship current affairs programme. Politics was always high on its agenda but it also covered other more mundane affairs. Like *TONIGHT*, the programme was a compilation of outside reports which were usually shot on film and studio interviews which usually took place live. As I have already mentioned, videotape had not yet made its debut. It was while I was working on *PANORAMA* that it was first seen in Britain.

I have already described how the American company Ampex had perfected tape technology more quickly than we did. In 1958, as the BBC was about to install its first American videotape machine, *PANORAMA* decided the Corporation's own attempts to master video technology should be revealed to the world. In April that year Richard Dimbleby appeared live on air in the Panorama studio. He was seated by a very large clock. He spoke for a couple of minutes about new ways of recording television programmes which were being pioneered, largely overseas. For the first time it would soon be possible to provide an instant playback of what had just taken place. As he explained what would happen live on air, he was simultaneously being recorded on Vera - the BBC's own prototype video recording apparatus, which was housed in a room down below. Dimbleby stopped speaking and pressed a button. A television screen in front of him burst into life and instantly replayed what we had just seen live. For the first time he had been able to demonstrate the advantages if instant playback. Television programmes would never be the same again.

That was not the only innovation I was to witness during my spell on PANORAMA. Please bear in mind that mobile phones and satellites had not been invented. We made telephone calls from our homes and offices or from Doctor Who type phone boxes which were to be found in almost every street. If we got connected, calls were often indistinct and difficult to hear. Calling Scotland from England took as long then as it does today to contact someone on the moon. I was thus not surprised when one day I was told that in the next edition of our programme we would be including an outside broadcast which would become a broadcasting milestone. We were to broadcast sounds and pictures live across the English channel !

As the great day approached our most powerful transmitter was shipped across to Calais with a *PANORAMA* camera crew. On the quay at Dover Richard and a small group of local celebrities assembled on the quay. As our programme started the great miracle occurred. Blurred but distinctly visible pictures arrived directly from France. We could see and hear someone saying "Bonjour" at exactly the same time in a foreign country over over twenty miles away. We felt as if we had landed on the moon!

Because *PANORAMA* often featured well known personalities and explored new frontiers in technology, audiences seemed to believe everything they saw and heard on the show. If it was on PANORAMA it must be true. In April 1957 we decided to put that to the test. One of our cameramen - Charles de Jaegher - recalled how at school he had been teased and told that spaghetti grew on trees. In 1960s England, while roast beef and two veg were fully understood, many dishes which were popular on the continent were less well known. One of those dishes was spaghetti, so we decided to have a laugh at our audiences' expense.

Under conditions of of great secrecy a film crew was sent to Switzerland to film a report on the spaghetti harvest there. It had been a mild winter and they were dealing with a bumper crop. Yards of wet spaghetti were draped over a number of trees and shot from various angles. Additional scenes were then shot in a pasta factory in St Albans in Hertfordshire. The treatment the film was given was completely straight. It was reported like any other news story. The commentary was read, with due gravitas, by Dimbleby himself.

It explained how in this small Swiss village they were struggling to cope as their spaghetti trees were weighed down with a bumper crop. A brilliantly conceived harvest scene was then staged. The film cost just over a thousand pounds to make. On 1st April it was duly transmitted as a normal *PANORAMA* news item. At the time it was estimated that 8 million people tuned in that night. The following day he BBC received hundreds of calls from people who wanted to know where they could buy a spaghetti tree!

From *PANORAMA* I was moved to light entertainment. My training course was now nearing its end and I was able to make a worthwhile contribution to the programmes I was asked to work on. I had gained a lot of experience working on live and filmed programmes with some of the best talents around. I had met lots of wonderful people and had survived a few disasters when things went wrong. Up to this point I only had a limited experience of working with actors but I knew that in light entertainment that situation was about to change.

I met the first of many stars I was work with over the next fifty years, at the Riverside Studios in Hammersmith in 1959. He was at the peak of his fame and when his shows were on television pubs emptied and people stayed at home to see what he was doing in his latest escapade. His name was Tony Hancock.

Hancock had started his career as a comedian but he came to fame in a radio show which was to launch many other famous names. His co star in the show was a ventroliqist's dummy - Archie Andrews. The show - *EDUCATING ARCHIE* was to launch the careers of Harry Secombe, Bruce Forsyth, Sid James and many other world famous names. The Scripts were written by a young Eric Sykes and various others who managed to capture the imagination of the nation in an extraordinary way. How a ventriloquist's show on radio managed to have such influence and power was quite beyond me but I was one of thousands of children who had paid to attend *ARCHIE ANDREW'S CHRISTMAS SHOW* at the Prince of Wales Theatre in my early days. I can still remember sitting in that huge theatre trying to see Peter Brough - who had stared his careers selling shirts - holding a small dummy on is knee and cracking jokes. *EDUCATING ARCHIE* was a huge success and Tony Hancock was one of the first to benefit from his connection with it.

After years of radio success Hancock eventually moved to television. Before I first met him he had done a series of television shows with the same title as his radio programmes - *HANCOCK'S HALF HOUR*. Tony played a struggling actor, who lived in dismal surroundings at 23 Railway Cuttings East Cheam, and dreamed of becoming a straight actor and a big star. It was a great character to play and his first BBC television series was a great success. Then commercial television came to Britain. The BBC was no longer the only broadcaster in the land.

Hancock had become an important national figure but, like many of the other stars I have worked with over the years he tended to forget that the character he played, which had brought him success, had been created for him. He had two of the best script writers television has ever known - Alan Simpson and Ray Galton. Simpson had started work as a shipping clerk the age of 19. Doctors then found he was suffering from tuberculosis. Galton was working for the Transport and General Workers Union when he contracted the same disease. He was 18 when the two first met a a sanatorium in Surrey which as being used as an isolation hospital. Several years later, when hey had both been released from hospital, they started writing scripts. What happened in the years after that is now enshrined in the history of world television.

The first series of *HANCOCK'S HALF HOUR,* which they wrote for BBC, was a great success but, like many comedians Hancock lacked self confidence. He always had doubts. When commercial television arrived in Britain he started to wonder if he would do better off if he left the BBC and went elsewhere. His Agent - Beryl Vertue - one of the best in the business, did not agree. The character his writers had created for him had captured the imagination of the nation and people wanted o know what was going to happen to him each week. When *HANCOCKS HALF HOUR* was being shown the streets were quiet and families stayed at home. The shows were produced by two men who was to teach me the most important lessons I ever learned about directing comedy for television. Duncan Wood and his colleague Dennis Main Wilson knew more about comedy than anyone except possibly David Croft, who I was to encounter much later on. Main Wilson had produced Hancock's radio shows Duncan Wood adapted them for television. He was a firm believer in a good script and once it had been approved he did not like it changed. Like me, he had started his career as a BBC Trainee. He was in radio, based in Bristol before he moved to television. Having worked in radio and television he knew what was required. He had worked with Benny Hill, which was not always the easiest of tasks, He understood the importance of timing and knew how to pace the speed of the action so dialogue would not be drowned out by laughter. He also knew exactly where to place his cameras and when they should move or stay put, Above all he liked to stick to a script and bring it to life, scene by scene and page by page.

Hancock was not particularly good at remembering his lines. Alcohol was beginning to take its toll though it had not yet become the major problem it was later to be. We were in the Riverside Studios in Hammersmith. As our show was transmitted live from our studio, it was simultaneously sent along a special telephone line to Lime Grove where it could be recorded on 16mm film for archive purposes.

Without those recordings many of Hancock's most memorable shows would have been lost for ever. On one occasion we knew things could be difficult from the moment Hancock arrived in his chauffeur driven car. It was immediately clear that all was not well. The day before, when he was being driven home, he had been involved in a minor accident. He was not seriously hurt but he was thrown through the windscreen and suffered concussion. He as still upset when he arrived next day. Wood and his team had been warned that it might be impossible to transmit that day but he had decided to proceed in the normal way. Overnight crews had built and lit the set and rehearsals has gone on all week in a drill hall nearby. Now it was time for the first run through.

We had got a few minutes in when Tony started to forget his lines. We stopped again and again and were clearly in trouble. Duncan called a break and we all moved away. Like most good Directors he had his own ways of dealing with people. Tantrums and rows were not for him.

As the crew started to light the next part of the set, he took Hancock aside. We watched as they moved to a quiet part of the studio where the previous day Duncan had arranged for something to be delivered. A curtain was raised and one of the first Autocue machines any of us had seen was revealed. It was not like the sophisticated products used today. It consisted of a canopy, a mirror and some huge sheets of yellow paper with perforated edges. A trained Autocue Operator, using a special giant typewriter, could type a script line by line on the yellow sheets which could then be moved up or down at a controlled speed. Hancock was mesmerised, as were we. Here was something entirely new. Later that day it was used for our transmission and, from that day on Hancock would never make another show unless an Autocue was present. The programme was transmitted on time and duly recorded, which was just a well because the episode we were doing that week was *THE BLOOD DONOR* - One of the most successful programmes Hancock ever made.

In the 1960s Hancock made two feature films which failed to take off as he had hoped. Their failure fuelled his doubts. He started to make his own decisions and ignore the advice of those who had made him a star. Fellow actors, who had played a key part in his television successes, were pushed aside. In 1962 he moved to commercial television and signed a contract with ATV. On paper the deal looked sound enough but there was one major snag which proved impossible to overcome, Simpson and Galton were under contract to the BBC and the Corporation would not let them write shows for Hancock if they were to be shown on ATV. Tony, who had started to drink far more than he should, ignored the issue and the contribution the writers had made to his career. ATV looked round for others to write his scripts. Several were found including the young an undoubtedly brilliant Eric Sykes, but they did not understand Hancock or the character he played. They had not created the little man from Railway Cuttings and could not get into the character to bring him alive. Other Writers were commissioned including Terry Nation, who wrote the first *DOCTOR WHO*, but the shows failed to take off.

Hancock eventually returned to the BBC. His biggest successes had all been written by Galton and Simpson but they had moved on. The BBC had asked them to write a script for for a programme in a new series which was to be called *COMEDY PLAYHOUSE*. The series would consist of a number of shows by different Writers with different casts. Galton and Simpson wrote a script which they called *THE OFFER*. It was about a couple of what were then known as rag and bone men, and it was to become one of their biggest successes under another name - *STEPTOE AND SON*. I will have more to say about that series later.

Hancock was to come came back into my life several years later. I was directing s film in Australia and working with an Australian crew. Like most Aussie crews, they were a pleasure to work with and we were getting on well when we came to a scene we could not get right.

It involved a car being driven along a road which passed under Sydney Harbour bridge. The script called for shots inside the car and more outside showing it approaching and passing by. It was mid summer and very hot. Inside the car an actor, our sound man the Cameraman and I were gasping for breath. The air conditioning had been turned off as it was spoiling the sound. We did a great many takes all of which ended with us stopping the car so makeup could patch up our actor who was dripping with sweat.

After yet another attempt to get things right, I called a halt and we stopped to get a cold drink. During the break our Camera Assistant, who had know my work in the UK, purchased a copy of the Sydney Morning Herald, which had just come out.

Didn't you know him?" He asked, thrusting the paper under my nose. And there it was. On an inside page, an article which had caught his eye. "English Actor Dead" was the heading. It reported that an empty bottle, some tablets and a note had been found alongside a body in a Bellvue Hill flat. Police had checked the identity of a middle aged man and discovered it was Tony Hancock. In his suicide note he had written his own obituary. It said "Things seemed to go wrong too many times". Television had lost a good man.

As my training neared its end I knew I would soon be fully qualified and on the BBC's full time staff. I had also been told I would be moving from being based at Lime Grove to the brand new Television Centre. I was about to reach another milestone in my life. I had enjoyed three wonderful years working with some of the best talents in the business. By keeping my mouth shut and my eyes and ears open I had managed to learn a lot more than I would have been able to do anywhere else in a much longer time. The Good Lord had looked after me and guided me well!

To celebrate my forthcoming move I thought I might throw caution to the winds and splash out a bit more than I would normally do. I was still living in the bed sitting room I had rented when I first moved to London. I was also driving a car I had bought at that time. In view of its age and condition I was surprised it had lasted so long. A complete lack of money, time and basic maintenance had taken its toll. I had bought it at a very smart garage on the outskirts of Ealing. I had gone there looking for the sort of car I knew I could not afford. After viewing every model they had on display I was about to go home and have a cup of tea when the lady in charge of secondhand sales came up to me. Miss Lazenby was an an unforgettable middle aged lady in a wide brimmed hat festooned with feathers. She knew exactly what she was doing and could spot a young man with expensive tastes and no money in three seconds flat. She had watched me traipsing round the showroom and realised she had a hopeless case on her hands. As I was about to go home she politely asked if I had found something I liked.

"Lots of things", I replied adding "But I think they are a little more expensive than I can afford at this week."Miss L. smiled. It was quite a shock, and then she added. "I think you might like to see a little gem I have just accepted in part exchange. If you like it we might be able to do a deal".

She lead me round the back of the showroom where the dustbins and crashed cars were usually kept. And there it was. A 1948 Morris Ten, with 130,000 miles on the clock and only twelve previous owners! Miss L liked her showroom to look smart and she did not like litter lying around. "If you like what you see and give me what I paid for it we could have a deal. "Of course" she added quickly "There will be no guarantee". " How much"? I asked. Her answer has remained indelibly printed in my mind to this day. Sixty eight pounds" she said triumphantly, and a deal was done!

I had more fun out of that car than any other vehicle I have ever owned. Years later. when I was running a multi-national production company, I got a new Jaguar every three years as it went with the job. It was good but it was never as much fun as my first set of wheels. My Morris Ten was an experience I would hate to have missed. In the days before MOT tests, when there was little traffic on the roads, it was a real experience to drive. You never knew what, if anything, was going to work. It burned almost as much oil as petrol and blue smoke came up through the floor from a leaky exhaust. The handbrake could only be trusted on level ground and the windows had to be wedged open or shut with wads of cardboard or paper. The windscreen wipers did work, if it wasn't raining, and the engine made a reassuring noise when it coughed into life. It was worth every penny I had paid for it. When I eventually decided it might be wise to sell, I put an advertisement in the London *Evening Standard.* A very pretty girl came to view and, after a test dive along a carefully chosen route, agreed to pay my asking price. It was - as you have probably guessed, sixty eight pounds!. As my purchaser prepared to drive away I again warned her that it was being sold as seen, with no guarantee. She gave me an enchanting smile and, as she drove away, added words which haunted me for days

"Don't worry," she exclaimed. My boyfriend will check it out. He's a Policeman!"

With a move to television centre imminent I thought it might be a good moment to invest in something which was a little bit smarter.

I had recently moved to a large Victorian house in a smarter part of Ealing. I had a double bedroom on the first floor above what I was told was a garage. For the first few months I was there no one went near it so I asked the housekeeper what it was used for. She explained that it contained a car which belonged to the man who owned the house. He now lived abroad and was hardly ever seen.

A few weeks later I happened to be going out when a very old man arrived and started to unlock the garage door. I wondered who he was, so I went over to make myself known. As the door swung open I was in for a surprise. There, in immaculate condition, was a 1938 Rolls Royce Park Ward limousine. It could have been new and had clearly been meticulously maintained but not used for years. The old man saw me looking and asked me to join him. "Are you interested in cars?" he asked, He could see that I was. "Not bad is it" he continued and then added. I don't use it any more but it used to be fun." He then showed me every detail of what had clearly been his pride and joy.

Finally I had to ask the obvious question. Who owns it now?"
"I do" he said adding before I could draw breath, "but it has got to be sold and I am not allowed to drive any more". The following day he asked if I would like to buy it. I explained that at my age a car like that would no doubt cost me a year's salary or more.

" You can have it for £5,000.00" he said "if you can settle before I go abroad." It must have been worth at least ten times that but I was under no illusions. It was way beyond my limits. The car remained where it was for several months until it was eventually towed away. I only wish I could have the same offer now!

After visiting my Bank Manager, who was now beginning to speak to me as my account was in credit, I decided to buy my first a new car on hire purchase. The first mini cars had just appeared and I went to look at one. It had a white roof and a pale blue body with the latest innovation - front wheel drive and I was soon convinced it would be a good buy for me.

As I had recently bought a 16mm film camera (A Bolex H16) I thought it might be fun if I could arrange to get a few shots of the factory where my car had been made. I decided to ring the manufacturers at their Longbridge factory which was near Birmingham and ask if it would be possible to take a few shots of the production line on which the car I had bought had been produced. They said they would see what they could arrange and a few days later I hired some rather heavy lights, which I just managed to get into the boot of my car, and set off for Longbridge.

When I arrived I stopped outside the main entrance and started to unpack. I was about to go into the building when a grey haired man wearing a sports jacket came over to me. Is this your car?" He asked. I admitted that it was. "And do you like it?" he continued. "It's wonderful I replied." My questioner seemed pleased and turned his attention to the lighting kit I had just removed from the car. "And you managed to get all that in the boot !" "Yes it was easy,"I replied, as indeed it was. "That's wonderful" my new friend concluded as he stretched out his hand. " My name Issigonis. Alec Issigonis. I work here. If you come inside I can show you where your car was made."

And that was how I met one of the greatest car Designers of the age. The man who designed the Morris Minor and then the first Mini. Without any security checks or formalities of any kind, he took me up to the office where he worked. It wasn't anything special. Just a large room with a drawing board at one end and a fairly modest desk.

On the right of his desk there were large windows through which he could see the main factory building, full of offices equipped with rows and rows of people at drawing boards, for this was before computers arrived on the scene. As I had my camera with me I asked if he would mind sitting at the desk and make a few sketches as if he was working on his designs. He did as I had asked as we continued to chat. That unique film had been lost until 2012 when I found it in my garage. Still frames from it are reproduced in this book for the very first time

After my day in Longbridge I returned to London to prepare to move to the new Television Centre. Before that move took place I had decided to take a short holiday. I had been working long hours for two and a half years and had enjoyed every moment but there comes a time when it is wise to take a break and for me that moment had come, but what should I do? I had been considering that question for quite a while. As my passion in life was making films, the decision I made was probably more predictable than I would have cared to admit. I decided it was time for me to go off and make a film on my own.

I had been working with teams of experienced professionals and using the best equipment available for months and had learned quite a lot. I had also bought a cheap film camera and wanted to know what it could do. With those things in mind I had been looking for a subject I felt I could make a film about. It had to be something or someone I could do justice to on a very low budget. It also had to be a subject I could shoot at weekends and on any days I could get off. Any equipment required would have to be cheap to hire and be small enough to fit into my car.

When those essential requirements had been met I hoped I might be able to find a subject which could potentially meet some other objectives. It would be nice if it could eventually make some money or at least recover its production cost. To do that I realised I needed a subject which was reasonably topical and of general interest.

When I was working on *MONITOR* I had got interested in the arts and had worked on a number of programmes on arts subjects. That experience and my own long term objectives pointed the way to the subject I decided to feature in my first film. At the time Coventry cathedral was front page news. It had been destroyed in the war and was now being being rebuilt to a controversial modern design.

The Architect - Sir Basil Spence - had commissioned a number of well known artists and craftsmen to produce works for the new cathedral. I thought the people he had selected might be good subjects for a film. One of those people was a New Zealander who had pioneered an entirely new way of doing giant glass engravings. I had seen some works he had done for the Shakespeare Memorial Trust at Stratford On Avon. They were very impressive but, as the glass he engraved was clear, I knew his work would be difficult to film. It would be a huge challenge to get it right but I wanted to see if what at first sight looked impossible might perhaps be done. I discovered that Hutton and his wife lived in St john's Wood and arranged to go and see them. Hutton was born in New Zealand . He had recently completed commissions on two P & O Ships - the liners Orsova and the first Oriana. When we first met he was working on the design which had won him his a huge commission to work on Coventry cathedral. I explained that I would like to film him working on the Coventry project and show some of the other work he had done. I then went on to give him some facts which I thought would end our conversation there and then. I explained that I was just completing a three year training course with BBC television but had never made a professional film on my own. I loved his work and would like to try to capture what he was doing on film. I did not have any money and could not pay a fee. All I could do was promise I would make every effort to do justice to what he was doing. If he disliked the end result it could be destroyed and that would be that. He listened to everything I had to say and then told me that if I rang him in a couple of days he would let me have his decision. Two days later Hutton and his wife agreed we should go ahead . Over the next few weeks we became good friends. As his work started to take shape I managed to get some useable film I was shooting in black and and white on outdated film stock to keep costs down. The camera I was using was powered by a clockwork motor which would only run one minute of film before it had to be wound up again. It was challenging work. When I completed my filming I hired a fully equipped cutting room to put it all together and used the skills I had learned to prepare a final soundtrack. I had just enough money left to ask a film laboratory to produce one copy of the final edited film.

John and Marigold Hutton liked what they saw and the comments of friends I showed it to were generally positive and helpful. They said it should get a wider showing but by then I was back at work at Television Centre and did know what to do. A colleague suggested I should send it to the Edinburgh Film Festival. As there was no entry fee I accepted his suggestion and *JOHN HUTTON - A FILM PORTRAIT*, as my first film was eventually called, was awarded a certificate of merit.. It had cost me £150.00 to produce.

From that point on things which were outside my control started to happen . A film and television distribution company, who had seen the film in Edinburgh, asked if they could act as my Sales Agents. A few weeks later the film was shown at a film festival in Toronto where it was awarded another certificate of merit. That showing resulted in a sale to Canadian television. Sales to Australia, New Zealand and various other countries followed and money started to roll in. A hundred and fifty pound production cost soon became fifteen hundred pounds profit and it went on from there. The success was all very gratifying but I feared it might cost me my job. My BBC contract specified that I was not allowed to make films or television programmes for any other network. My first film had already been bought by three overseas television networks but the biggest threat to my future came from much nearer home. The BBC had a programme purchasing department. Unbeknown to me they had bought award winning films from a number of international film festivals to form the basis of a programme they were planning to screen when they opened their new network- BBC2. My Hutton film was one of the titles they had acquired. Fortunately they did not immediately connect it with me. The film eventually produced a good profit so I thought it might be worth trying to make a sequel along similar lines. This time I decided to focus on another artist who had been involved at Coventry. John Piper was an even bigger name and his multi-coloured baptistery window had caused a great stir when it was first unveiled. In my second film *JOHN PIPER- A FILM PORTRAIT* I looked at his work at Coventry and at cathedrals in Liverpool and Chichester which he was also deeply involved in. That film was was premiered at the National Film Theatre in London and then shown all over the world. In 2012 both the films I have mentioned were digitally restored and re-edited to make one composite film which has now been released on DVD under the title of *GREAT ARTISTS REDISCOVERED*. It includes rare shots of both men working on their biggest projects and is a fitting tribute to two great artists who, alas, are no longer with us.

FROM THE ARCHIVES

Programme 6

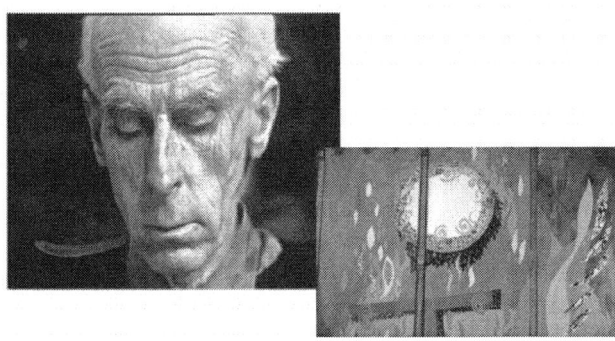

GREAT ARTISTS

JOHN PIPER

JOHN HUTTON

As I was shortly to leave Lime Grove and venture a few hundred yards up the road to Television Centre, I though I would splash out and boost the area's retail trade by making a purchase I had put off making for far too long. Though I had now worked in television for several years I still did not own a television set. I never watched at home and at work everywhere we went we were surrounded by the most expensive and up to date sets. I had got used to being without a box to goggle at. My parents had never owned a set either - a fact I conveniently forgot to mention at my first job interview. When I left home and moved to London that situation had remained unchanged. My parents did not get one until I had been working in the industry for some time. My father always preferred the wireless because he knew where all the control buttons were and what kind of programmes to expect.

A few minutes walk from Lime Grove there was a shop with very large windows which were always packed with televisions. They were all second hand ex rental sets. As I did not expect to be at home long enough to watch anything much I thought one of those would suit me. In those days sets only showed small pictures in black and white but the sets themselves were sometimes splendid affairs. They were made with good quality highly polished wood and could look very smart indeed. I sought a salesman's advice and agreed to buy a set he thought would be the right one for me.

That night I took it home to my Ealing bed-sit. I plugged it in and switched on the power. It burst into life. There was a picture, of sorts, and what was probably sound but my attention was distracted by a knock at the door. I opened it to find the housekeeper standing with the mop she never seemed to be parted from. She was accompanied by a man in a blue uniform.

"Ah! Mr Burder, I'm glad you're back. This is Mr Timmins. He is visiting all our Tenants. He's from TV licensing and he would like to check the number on the licence for your set." My newly acquired set was crackling away in the background as she spoke.

" Well" I started to explain. "I don't have a licence. I have only just bought the set. In fact I only switched it on a few minutes ago". The Inspector grinned. "They all say that sir. To save time if you just let me have your full name and date of birth I will include it in my report." What else could I say!

The following day I was at our local post office when it opened to buy what I should have ben able to produce the previous day. I knew it was probably too late. I also knew the BBC took a very dim view view of staff who did not have a television licence, so my whole career could be on the line. For the next few weeks I checked every post as it arrived. I was expecting to receive a summons but, much to my surprise, it never came. My anxiety lasted longer than the set which died three weeks after I had brought it home.

The new BBC Television Centre at White City, Shepherds Bush in west London opened in 1961. It was a brilliantly designed landmark building in just the right place. It was easy to reach. White City underground station, with a direct link to the heart of central London, was a hundred yards away. Most of the major buildings the BBC used at that time were easy to reach by road, rail and public transport. Inside its doors the Centre had almost everything any programme maker could want to find. It had had cost ten million pounds to build and the money had been wisely spent. Ask anyone who, like me, had the good fortune to work there what TVC was like and they will give you positive reports. It had a special atmosphere which made it a great place to work and, in the relatively short time it was allowed to function without the intervention of of politicians, cost accountants and other so called "experts" who should have known better, it helped the BBC to remain a world leader in television programming.

The circular shaped building ,usually referred to by staff as "the Doughnut", housed all the main departments needed to make television programmes under one roof. Studios, offices, workshops, storage areas, a canteen and many other key areas could be reached on foot in minutes by simply walking round the building. Sets could be designed, built and equipped on site and of any props required could usually be found in the props store. Shows either went out live from the 15 studios in the building or were recorded on video or film or projected from Telecine in suites located at various points. The building was designed to save time and money and, when it as efficiently managed, that is what it did.

I was there in its early years, when our main interest was in making good programmes and long before accountants and focus groups, who knew little or nothing about television production, were let loose. We did what the building had been designed to do.

Each of the 15 studios included in the original development was planned with a different purpose in mind. The biggest - Studio One (TC1) was vast. It could accommodate huge sets and, if it was required, a full symphony orchestra alongside. It was used to televise operas, large scale drama productions and light entertainment shows. The two studios next door (TC2 and TC3) were smaller but still large enough to be used for major programmes.

They were usual*ly occupied by dramas.* Series or shows like *Z CARS*, *STEPTOE AND SON* and *FAWLTY TOWERS* were among the many programmes which originated there. There were also a number of smaller studios, used for shows like THE *SKY AT NIGHT*, and a presentation suite where regional and national programmes were linked and introduced. When the first phases of the development were all up and running the BBC decided to move its television news operation from Alexandra Palace, where it had originally started and was still running, to television centre. A new wing (The Spur") was built to house all the additional a departments required. For the first time all the main BBC television news and programme production departments were now under one roof. And that is how it should have remained.

When I moved into television centre for the first time I was confident that it would see me out at the end of my career. I was young. It was new and I was working with some of the best people in the business. What could possibly occur to change that? For several years I had a wonderful time working on great programmes in what subsequently proved to be the golden age of British television. I had completed my training course but I continued to learn. Working with some of the greatest talents the industry has ever known it was impossible to do otherwise. I just had to take in what was happening around me.

In studio one *DOCTOR FINLAY'S CASEBOOK* was being rehearsed for transmission that night. The first of a series, it included several film sequences which had been shot Scotland. The programme was based on books written by A.J. Cronin. The series was popular but Cronin did not like the scripts. He complained that new characters he had not created were being introduced. His intervention caused quite a stir when a national newspaper had got hold of a copy of his complaint and suggested the series might be taken off the air. At Television Centre that matter, like many others issues concerning productions staged there over the years, was resolved without any major conflict.

A week later the same studio was being used for *STEPTOE AND SON*. I wanted to see how it progressed because it was being written by two scriptwriter I had been first encountered in my Hancock days - Alan Simpson and Ray Galton. It was being produced by Duncan Wood who had taught me so much when I was working with him and Hancock on *THE BLOOD DONOR* at the Riverside Studios in Hammersmith. On that occasion I had seen how good he was at handling artistes who could be temperamental - a quality every good Producer needs to posses. You will recall that on the day our show was due to be transmitted Hancock was recovering from a car accident the previous day and was finding it difficult to rem*ember his lines until an Autocue was produced. On* STEPTOE he also had problems to sort out. The two stars of the show were not the best of friends. The younger Steptoe was played by Harry H Corbett - a fine actor who was married, had children and was used to playing serious parts. His co star - Wilfrid Brambell - was a brilliant actor too but temperamentally the two men were poles apart. Brambell was character actor who often played older men. He was also a gay alcoholic and well know for his tantrums and outrageous behaviour. On set, when the programmes went out live and later on when they were recorded as if it was a live transmission, all seemed sweetness and light. They brought brilliant scripts to life so well the programmes won awards and captured the hearts of the nation. But the production team often had to deal with difficult issues which were not in the script. Watching them, at work I saw how difficult things could be. I don't think they loathed each other, as some later press reports tended to suggest. My impression was that they were totally incompatible and both felt trapped by their commitment to play roles they did not enjoy. When each show ended and went off the air, Brambell would be off as quickly as he could get away. When crew and and cast met again to start work on the next show he could be reticent and unhelpful refusing to rehearse in character until the very last moment. The atmosphere was tense because no one could ever be sure what would happen next. Corbett and Brambell finally fell out completely when they were doing a stage show tour in Australia in 1976. Brambell's alcohol problem had by then become acute. On one occasion he did not turn up at all, leaving Corbett to go on stage alone. They toured Australia in separate cars and only met on stage. They never worked together again. Both have now died, which is a great loss to the acting profession.

Television Centre quickly became the BBC's main production Hub. The success of the Centre can be gauged by the programmes that were produced there. They included many of Britain's most popular television shows. Titles which were popular at home and sold overseas. It was a privilege to have had been able to work there.

Today programmes are made by many companies and shown by lots of different television networks. Viewers have a bewildering choice. In the year when Television Centre opened, a large percentage of the programmes shown by the Corporation were actually produced by the BBC. Many were made on BBC premises by BBC staff or people who were paid by them. Today the facilities they used and those very experienced production teams are no longer there. Television today is all all about making money. Programmes have to be produced at minimal cost. If possible - and many programme Commissioners give this point far too much emphasis - they should be able to generate income from the moment they first go on air. In practical terms that means that if audiences are invited to participate by phoning in on premium rate lines the company transmitting the shows will get an immediate cash benefit. Phone lines for competitions and quiz shows generate cash and there are others who can also benefit more than the viewers. Talent shows are easier and cheaper to stage than dramas or series of situation comedies. They do not require actors who need to be experienced and have to be paid. Someone who can't sing but is willing to try on a talent show may be happy to appear for nothing or for a minimal fee. If he or she manages to appeal to viewers, they may be offered a short term contract. Any offer will probably not come from the company transmitting the show. It is more likely to come from an Agent who can exploit the recently discovered talent and earn good fees and a high rate of commission. When that talent has been exploited or exhausted the Agent and the television company can look elsewhere. There are good Agents and good talent shows but there are many more prepared to profit from vulnerable people and leave them feeling they have been fooled. The key point I want to make is that the BBC used to have wonderful facilities and a host of people under contract who had well proven track records and a lot of different talents. If you see a BBC show today there is a good chance it will have been made "outside". The programme may include a credit reading "Executive Producer for the BBC," or some equally worthless accolade. That will probably simply mean that the hard working people who wrote the script and shot, edited and recorded the programme, will have had to put up with some salaried individual (probably with some worthless degree) who has put his or her oar in at various points. He or she may have little or no experience of actually doing what he or is now being credited with, but has made fatuous comments at every stage and and ensured that what is being done is politically correct. So why are the resources and opportunities which used to be there not available today?

To understand the answer to that question we need to recall what was happening at the BBC in 1986. Then British television was in its prime. The BBC and commercial companies were doing well but the country was facing difficult times. We had survived the industrial turmoil of a miners strike and a three day week. For the first time in its history the BBC's Director General was an experienced programme maker. He was Alasdair Milne - an enormously gifted man who, with Tony Essex had been my Producer when I worked *TONIGHT* After that he had gone on to supervise the production of *THE GREAT WAR* - one on the finest documentary series anyone has ever produced. Milne did brilliantly but then politics intervened and Margaret Thatcher became Prime Minister. Mrs Thatcher did not like the way he had handled the industrial unrest which had plagued the country for months. When she should have taken a back seat, she intervened. The BBC has always been a prime target for disgruntled politicians and it still is today. They do not like an autonomous organisation which is not a commercial company or government government owned. It is and has always been fiercely independent. Anyone who doubts the value of that only needs to spend a week or so watching television in America, where we news reports and almost everything else are heavily influenced by commercial or political pressures. The Thatcher

Government did not like opposition and the Prime Minister lost no time in making her views known. Milne stood by what he had said. Behind the scenes, Mrs Thatcher arranged for a more easy going public figure - who those working for the BBC instantly recognised and described as a "hatchet man" - to be appointed as Chairman of the Governors of the BBC. In that position Marmaduke Hussey did what he was told and shortly after his appointment Alasdair Milne resigned.

Milne's departure was big blow to the freedom of the press and the BBC's independence. For the first time, politics had influenced a key appointment in a national broadcasting organisation. Hussey eventually replaced Milne with a new Director General - Michael Checkland - an Accountant who had been head of the Corporation's central finance section for some time. As he would probably be the first to admit, his knowledge of the many processes involved in making television programmes would not fill many volumes. It was not his world. As a thoroughly decent and hard working man he did his best but the Prime Minister wanted more. The appointment was then announced of a man who had prepared a report for Mrs Thatcher on the future strategy for British television,. He was know to be sympathetic to her views. His name was John Birt and his appointment changed BBC Television for ever more. When the appointment was announced Mr Birt's arrival produced very different reactions from those working in the BBC and others who also had an interest in the future of British television. Optimists drew attention to the fact that the Corporation's recent accounts had shown an enormous budget deficit and that situation had to be fixed. Birt had worked successfully for Granada Television but his appointment as BBC Director General on a freelance consultancy basis, caused controversy. Salaried BBC staff did no longer felt safe and they doubted his ability to manage a national institution

Birt spent seven years restructuring the ways in which the BBC ran its business. Some of his ideas were undoubtedly improvements on what had been going on before. Others were too radical. They upset many people and ended well established practices which had been in use for years. Probably the biggest innovation - and in many minds the most disastrous of all - was what he called " Producers choice." In its simplest form that meant that programme makers would have the power to buy services from outside the BBC. That huge decision made many of the corporations's facilities and staff redundant almost overnight. BBC Producers soon found that the internal cost of facilities and personnel they had used in the past were now much higher than they would be if they made their productions"outside"

The full effect of this policy decision took a while to assess but in a few months it was obvious that many of the facilities the BBC had built up and treasured for years, would not be used again at their new price. The whole business of assessing a programme's production costs and allocating resources to make it had been turned upside down. And that is why Television Centre was eventually forced to close. The repercussions of those times are still being felt today

When my BBC training was drawing to a close one of my last attachments was to one of the outposts of the BBC empire. It wasn't actually very far away. It was in Shepherd's Bush, just up the road from most of the other departments it was supposed to deal with. It had originally been known as the transcription unit. In radio days it was responsible for transcribing and distributing copies of programmes produced overseas. As an afterthought in later years their brief had been extended and they were now also allowed to transcribe BBC programmes and send them overseas. By the time I joined the unit it had been renamed. It was now BBC Enterprises and its primary task when I was there was to sell and distribute BBC programmes abroad. It was a small department by BBC standards. Producers did not like it because they were asked to do things they did not want to do. Retakes for scenes which has just been recorded so preparing versions for sale overseas would be easier. Music and effects soundtracks, free of English dialogue so shows could be dubbed in other languages. Producers saw that as a additional burden from which they would not benefit at all. Enterprises was thus given a low priority In time it has established itself and now does an excellent job in making the BBC's many excellent productions known around the world, but it was not always so.

It was while I was attached to Enterprises I got involved with one of the most prestigious programmes the BBC produced. It was made every year and it was always handled by "the men at the top".That usually meant the Head of Outside Broadcasting or whatever department was going to be most involved. It should have been the simplest show of the year to set up and make but, in view of its cast, it was blown up out of all proportions. It only had one star but God himself could not have caused more panic. Our star, as you have probably, guessed was Her Majesty The Queen.

In those days The Queen's Christmas message was filmed way before Christmas. In the year I was involved it was recorded in Buckingham Palace . Her Majesty, in the early part of her reign had been quite a nervous performer. Surrounded by the BBC hierarchy I can understand why! She soon became a master of the techniques involved and is now a relaxed and brilliant performer. The procedure for making the programme was straightforward enough. It was shot at the Palace. It was then taken by a motorcycle despatch rider to a film laboratory at Finsbury Park in north London, where it was processed. It was then returned to us to be edited. I was working in the cutting room concerned that year when what should have been a perfectly routine did not go according to plan.

I doubt if Her Majesty has ever been told about what happened that week but if she has not, and is reading this book, she will be able to find out now! Editing the film was the easiest job imaginable. The Queen usually got everything right first time . If she or someone else decided there was something which might be improved, a section of the speech might have been retaken and that retake would have to be cut in. It was a five minute job. In the year I was involved everything had gone according to plan. The programme was recorded and processed and returned to our cutting room. Today that building has become a hotel but it was then a block of preview theatres and cutting rooms. The Television Theatre, where less heralded performances were produced ever week, was at the other end of Shepherd's Bush Green just up the road.

We cut the film in about half an hour and the sent our edited master copy back to the laboratory so copies could be made for television stations around the world. They were produced in conditions of strict security, under senior management supervision, and delivered by hand to the BBC. We then prepared for them to be sent to television networks around the world. Each copy had to be accompanied by a letter from Buckingham Palace. On the Palace's headed notepaper paper it decreed that the enclosed film must mot be shown before 0900 hours GMT on Christmas day. Films and letters were then packed ready for despatch by special courier or in the diplomatic bags of the countries concerned.

It was as simple as that. In an ideal world everything would go according to plan but in everyday life that doesn't always happen. As our week ended, films and letters were sent out and we went off for a weekend at home after all our strenuous efforts. It was on the Monday morning that the alarm was raised.

A few days before the Royal broadcast had been edited an ex BBC employee had visited the cutting rooms to see the colleagues he had once worked with. He had brought with him an exceptionally blue film which he had reluctantly agreed to leave for the weekend so it could be seen by people who were working on later shifts. With the Royal Message in production the blue movie was temporarily forgotten. When its owner returned on Monday morning, to everyone's dismay, the copy he had left could not be found. We tore the place apart and looked everywhere. As the day passed a really dreadful possibility began to dawn. Perhaps someone had put the wrong film in the wrong can. If that had happened, we knew that somewhere in the world there must be a film can containing a very blue movie, accompanied by a sealed letter from Buckingham Palace. As the letter specified the film must not be shown until Christmas day it seemed that someone somewhere could be heading for a shock. The possibilities were too awful to consider or discuss and no one seemed to know what should be done. For several days we sweated and prayed then, just as a full confession was about to be made, the missing film turned up. A technician from another department had borrowed it and failed to tell anyone what he had done!

When my training ended I became a fully qualified member of the BBC's staff and worked on many of the programmes I have included in my list of those which were produced at Television Centre. It was a great time to be there and I would not have missed it for the world. I was just in my thirties and knew I had the rest of my life ahead to pursue a career. I had already got further than I ever thought I would and did not really worry about what would happen next. I did not have to do anything . I could just stay put and continue as I was. I was being well paid and working with many of the best talents in the business, so there was no rush to reach a decisions of any kind.

Since I had joined the Corporation as a Trainee, the television industry had changed a lot. Commercial television was now up and running and doing great things. The BBC was still generally considered to be the leader of the pack nationally and internationally but things were changing there too. As as insider I was more aware of what those changes were likely to mean than others outside would probably have been. I have already described some of the changes at the top. New Chairmen of Governors and new Director Generals. I have also mentioned that politicians had started to try to take control. They had succeeded in arranging a number of appointments but the BBC still remained independent of government control. It still is today and,if that ever ends and it becomes a government department or a company run by one of the the so called "Captains of Industry," it would be a disaster for us all. It has its faults but it is still so much better than the national broadcasters in most other countries. It now has, and welcomes healthy competition from Channel 4, which makes many excellent programmes, and has provided a stimulus which the BBC needed. Other commercial companies have done brilliant things too. Some have themselves been spoiled by governmental or commercial pressures. Granada Television and Yorkshire Television both made first class programmes. One no longer exists and the other is a shadow of what it used to be, but it is still there and doing a great job and that is good for British television as a whole.

Today independent companies (usually referred to simply as "Indies") really have most of the power. Programmes shown on terrestrial and satellite networks are now often made by "Indies" - Independent programme makers who are either commissioned by a network to make shows for them or originate their own material and then sell it either as one off programmes or as a series to whoever will buy. If you think you might like to work in television or make films for a living there are a number of points you should consider before you make even your first move in whatever direction you think could be right for you.

On the cover of this book the main title is - "How to be a Film Producer". I did that because I remembered how helpful books were to me when, as a very young man, I first thought about the industries I eventually chose to join. I knew no one who worked in film or television and nothing about what working in the industries I was interested in actually involved. I did go cinemas and enjoyed amateur photography but that was about all I knew, so I started to borrow books. They told me what I needed to know and encouraged me to make decisions which eventually changed the course of my life.

In this book I have so far recalled a a few of the experiences I have had in my chosen career. I hope you may have found them interesting. Perhaps I have described situations you would like to have been involved in. If that is the case, the rest of the book should fill in any gaps and help you to choose and succeed in the career that is right for you.

If you are still at school or college you will need to make some decisions quite early on. If you are already doing a different kind of job, have become bored or think it may be time for a change, you also need to make some decisions. I may be able to help you to make decisions which are right for you and steer you away from goals which might lead you astray. I have been lucky enough to have a long, enjoyable and successful career. I have worked in the industry for around fifty years.

I am still learning but I have acquired enough knowledge to help those who now share the ambitions I once had. In the pages which follow I shall endeavour to pass on a few tips I have learned over the years. They will not teach you everything. You may learn nothing, but they should at least encourage you to think about things you need to consider, and not waste time and money going the wrong way.

When I had completed my BBC training I knew a lot more about the technicalities of production that I had done when I was lucky enough to be accepted for the course. I then had to make another decision. Did I want to stay with the BBC as a permanent member of staff, or would it be wise to go elsewhere? I could have gone to commercial television. I had already had several invitations to join people I had worked with who had made that move. Alternatively I could just stay put and continue what I was doing, which I enjoyed very much. And there was a third option. I could start out on my own, working as a freelance technician - probably as a Cameraman, an Editor or eventually, when I had gained more experience, directing as an individual or as a member of an independent production team. Those were the decisions I faced at that point and, if you are starting out today you will have to make much the same decisions.

First you will need some training to acquire essential basic skills. So how can you go about that and what opportunities are now open to you ?

Alas there is no quick way of acquiring knowledge. It and experience go hand in hand. If you have no basic training which is relevant to what you want to do, you may be able to speed things up by borrowing the sort of equipment you are interested in and conducting your own experiments, as I did at school. There I borrowed my Housemaster's movie camera. It was basic and old but using it I learned about exposures, focus and lenses - three important skills.

If you produce a simple film which shows what you can do, it can act as a showcase to start your career. You don't have to remake *GONE WITH THE WIND* on a student loan to impress people who can help you succeed.

Film making is an infectious disease. Those of us who catch it find it is hard to resist and can be incurable. We get ideas for subjects we are desperate to film. We eventually learn, often the hard way, that it is unwise to to attempt to make films we cannot afford to make properly. I have always found that the best option of all is to make the sort of films other people will pay you to make. That may mean filming subjects which are not at the top of your list of priorities but it could save you a lot of cash. You can also thoroughly enjoy doing it, as I have done for many years. With the exception of two films I made in my student days, all the films I have produced have made money, and there are not many people who can claim that. I have either been paid to make them or they have been films on subjects which proved to be commercially viable, so they recovered their costs. The first of those options is by far the best. Films which prove to be commercially viable are games of chance. We can all convince ourselves that the next film we want to make is going to be a smash hit. On paper it may look sound enough but, as many impoverished film makers have learned to their cost, things don't always go according to plan. If you get your money up front, before you start, you will know where you are. You will need to build a profit margin into your costs and you should try to retain overall control on how the film is made. I have spent a lot of my film making career making films which have been paid for by industrial and commercial sponsors. It has given me a great deal of pleasure and brought me considerable rewards. If you think you might like to do the same I will give you a few hints on what you could do.

You do not have to buy the best professional gear to learn how to use it. There are equipment hire companies which specialize in film and television work. They hire out basic and elaborate gear by the day or for whatever length of time their customers require. If you decide to opt for full time training, you will need to find a company, a film school or a university which runs a suitable course.

As I mentioned earlier in this book, you need to be careful when making your choice. There are good schools and bad ones and the same is true of most of the organisations which claim to provide media training of one kind or another. Here are some of the pitfalls you should try to avoid. The first thing to check is the curriculum for any course you are thinking of joining. Does it cover things you need to know? Or has it been compiled by people who have included as many topics as they can to make the course longer so they can charge more? Four weeks on a well planned practical course will do you more good than three years on one which includes topics which no one is going to give you plus points for. Are the subjects ones which any potential employer you approach is likely to be interested in? He or she will want to know if your training has given you the sort of skills they are looking for. And what of the organisation running the course. It it well established and staffed by people who currently work in the industry or have only recently retired? Is the equipment you will use up to date or are you being taught to use gear which the school bought cheaply many years ago? Who are your fellow students going to be? Are they like you you or are they mostly from overseas? If the latter is true they may be on grants. That may suit the school very well but do they really want to be there? Are film or television their passions in life, or was the prospect of spending time in Britain with all expenses paid the main reason why they are where they are? Is English their first language or will your studies be slowed down because every point has to be made a number of times before it is understood?

Whatever training organisation you are considering, check its track record before you get involved. Ask past students if they were able to acquire knowledge they needed to get worthwhile jobs, or are they stacking shelves in their local supermarket? Track them down and ask what they thought. Do they feel they have been helped or have they simply wasted a year or more? Use social media to contact people who have done what you propose to do .A little basic research early in the day can save you a lot of heartache and expense later on. If you decide a training course is not right for you, or if it is too expensive to afford, that is not the end of the world. I may even prove to be a blessing in disguise.

One of the best alternative ways of starting a media career is to try to get a job straight away. Any job will show that you are employable and, from an employer's point of view, any track record is better than none.

If you are lucky or clever enough to persuade a film or television company to offer you even a basic position you may find that taking it proves to be a wise move. It will depend on you. If you are a disaster, of course it will not. If you are smart, hard working and willing to learn, you could be at the start of a great career. They will not welcome you with open arms. You will be one of hundreds of people wanting to do what you hope to achieve. But don't give up! If you are able, enthusiastic and hard working you will get there in the end. I did, and if I can so can you!

When you have acquired some basic qualifications, or if you feel a training course is not for you, you will need to co make decisions on some other issues. Once you are sure that career in film and/or television is really what you really want to do, you will need to define your ambition rather more precisely. You will find that is easier if you first ask yourself a simple question. In settling for the career you have chosen, what *exactly* is your ultimate goal? Do you expect to make a fortune and possibly become a millionaire? Or are you happy to earn enough to enjoy a good standard of living and settle for that? Do **you** want to do?

Do you want to operate from one particular base or do you want to travel round the world? When I decided to leave the BBC I had to decide what to do and I then considered each of those points. It took me some time to resolve them all but the decisions which charted my future course can be summed up in a few lines.

I wanted to earn a good living but did to expect to end up being a millionaire.

I wanted to travel and see the world, preferably with someone else footing the bill!

Enjoyment of a life, without hassle or worries, was most important of all.

Perhaps you share some or all of these goals? If you do, in the pages which follow you will find out how I set out to achieve them and what I learned on the way.

When you are sure you want to build a career in film or television you can start to plan you route to the top. You know you want to make films or television programmes. Now you need to be more precise. What sort of films to you want to be involved in? If television is your prime target, do you see yourself producing complete programmes or advertising commercials? You can make a lot of money making a 30 second commercial and lose (or occasionally make) a lot of money making much longer films. Perhaps you want to make feature films for showing in cinemas or on line. Or would you be wiser to consider a less publicised market which can also produce rich rewards. Making sponsored films for what is known on the industry as "non theatric showing" can produce a lot of cash and take you round the world. Non theatric audiences simply means people like you and me who watch films at home on their computers, at school or wherever they happen to be. The crucial point is that they do not have to pay an entrance fee to sit and view in a particular place. Many commercially sponsored films are produced for non theatric showing and that is an vast area which you would be unwise to ignore. We will explore it in detail in the course of this book.

Let's start with network television programmes. As I have already mentioned, in the UK most of those shows used to be made by the BBC or ITV companies. They are now also made by a host of independent companies ("Indies"). If you have the right qualifications you can apply to work for them and join one of their production teams. There is no reason why you should not be able to succeed and have a great career. If you join a large organisation like the BBC, you may find you have to wait quite a long time to get to the top. When I had completed my training and worked for the BBC for several years, I realised that if I wanted to get a senior position it was going to take a while. As a young man I did not want to wait.

A few months or a couple of years would have been alright, but to move from Editor to Producer was going to take longer than I was prepared to wait. Like many before me, I found it was quicker to resign my staff position and move "outside". I could then produce programmes which the BBC and other networks could buy if they wished. It was a gamble. I might simply have been out of a job, but it worked for me and opened the door to a lot of opportunities I might otherwise have missed.

I was also free to accept commissions to make shows for them as an outside contractor, which I subsequently did. That is what I and many of my colleagues in the BBC at that time thought was best, and it proved to be a sound move for me. Working like that will not give you the long term security you get with a permanent staff job. You will not be presented with a clock or an illuminated scroll when you have done your job for 25 years, but you will be able to enjoy more freedom and make some money.

If you decide you want to make feature films you need to be aware that you are entering a high risk business. It may It look glamorous from the outside but if you want a secure long term future, read the small print before you step inside. Feature films are usually one off ventures. Raising the finance to make a feature can often take years. Assembling a crew to make it, once funds have been found and an acceptable script produced, also takes time. Most of the people who will make that film will not be paid while it is being set up. When shooting starts they may be OK but features are always risky ventures and, compared to television programmes, relatively few are made.

The third type of production I mentioned - sponsored films for non theatric use - gets much less publicity but it can give you an enjoyable and profitable career. It is not in the least glamorous. You are unlikely to find Brad Pitt or Steven Spielberg working on a sponsored film, but it can offer you regular employment And, if you know what you are doing, you can make a lot of money. You can travel round the world with someone else paying, as I have been fortunate enough to do many times.

If you are interested in starting a business on your own or with friends and colleagues it can provide you with sound foundations to build on. As this book progresses we will see what that kind of work actually involves.

I made my first commercially successful film when I was 24. It was my documentary on the work of Artist John Hutton, which I described earlier in this book. It was not intended to be a commercial production. I was in the middle of my BBC training course at the time so it had to be shot at weekends and on my days off. As my contract specifically forbade me to make films commercially or for anyone else, I had to keep quiet about what I was doing in my own time. It was only when the film had been finished and was selected for showing at a couple of international film festivals that word of its existence was publicly announced. Eventually, as I mentioned earlier, the BBC bought the finished film from a sales agent and it became one of the first films ever shown on BBC2. It went on to bring in ten times more than it had cost to make, which surprised no one more than me! I had scraped and saved to buy enough film stock to shoot and process the shots I felt needed to to make the film work. I edited it at night in a professional cutting room which the owners did not use out of normal working hours. It was shot on the most basic equipment and was really intended to tell me if I had or had not acquired enough skills to make anything worthwhile. I learned a lot more lessons making that film. I had been taught the basic rules on writing scripts. I knew what cameras could do and how they could be controlled. Lighting equipment and techniques were no longer entirely new to me and I knew enough about sound to know what kind of sounds I would need and how they could be used to bring scenes to life. Knowing what to shoot is vital when you are making any film. In the trade it is known as "how to cover a story".Every television Reporter and film crew needs to know how to cover any assignment he or she may be sent to film. If you don't get the right shots you will not have a story. If you get the wrong shots you may not be able to put them together.

Gaps and deficiencies will immediately become obvious in a cutting room. In the pages which follow I will try to give some guidance on this very very important issue. One of the important lessons the Hutton film taught me was that in choosing a subject to film you have to pick one which can be properly covered with the equipment and resources you have available. Today I am often asked to go and talk to students in film schools, universities and elsewhere. I always say I would prefer to go and listen to what the students have to say and want to know. They all have their own ideas and ambitions, which I think that is wonderful. They come from a different age and a different world but but we get on well and, by sharing our experiences and ambitions I generally manage to pass on the odd tip or two in the course of a day. I am always interested in what students are doing. As part of their courses many are given a limited budget to make a film. Most turn out creditable results but the point which always surprises me is how ambitious some of their ideas are. Science fiction dramas and stories which require large casts and lots of locations often feature in their plans. Those who opt for simple subjects and treatments which they can do justice to with limited resources, generally find they have less problems and end up with money in the bank. If you produce a simple film which shows what you can do, it can act as a showcase to start your career. You do not have to make a major epic on a student loan to impress people who can help you succeed. At the end of this book I have suggested a few simple types of film you may care to try to make as your show reel. They do not require extensive resources or loads of cash. And they could give you a chance to practice your skills and see what you can do.

That may mean filming subjects which are not top of your list of priorities but it could save you a lot of cash. You can also thoroughly enjoy doing it, as I have done for many years. With the exception of two films I made in my student days, all the films I have produced have made money, and there are not many people who can claim that. I have either been paid to make them or they have been films on subjects which have proved to be commercially viable, so they recovered their costs. The first of those options is by far the best. Films which prove to be commercially viable are games of chance. We can all convince ourselves that the next film we want to make is going to be a smash hit. On paper it may look sound enough, but as many impoverished film makers have learned to their cost, things don't always go according to plan. If you get your money up front, before you start, you will know where you are. You will need to build a profit margin into your costs and you should try to retain overall control of how your film is made. I have spent a lot of my film making career making films which have been paid for by industrial and commercial sponsors. I have had a wonderful time and they have brought in considerable rewards. If you think you might like to do the same, I will give you a few hints on what you could do.

So, what do sponsors want? I can hear you asking yourself that question. To get the right answer you first need to consider what films can do. You may care to try and answer that yourself before reading the next paragraphs, in which I will then suggest what you may or may not have included in your list.

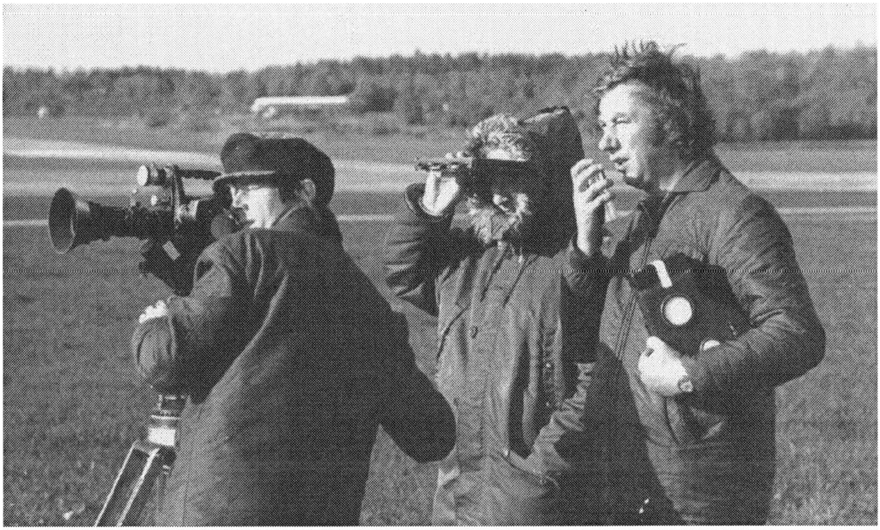

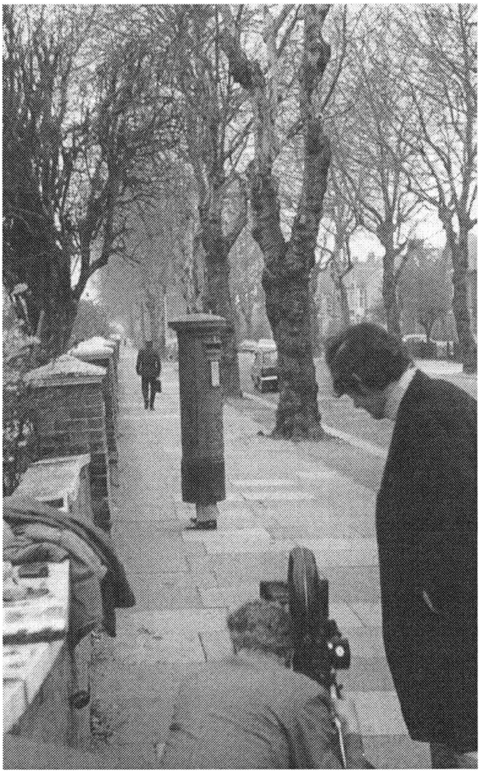

So let's see if you did, or did not, pick the money spinners.

Films can entertain. For feature films and some television productions, that is their main aim in life but they will always have a secondary aim and that may well be a deciding factor. They will need to make money. They are also likely to be expensive to produce. If you are going to make musicals, dramas or comedy series you will probably end up with a sizeable cast of performers and quite a large production team. You may also need sets, costumes and, in the case of dramas in particular, often costly special effects. It can be challenging and fun and the rewards can be great but you will need substantial financial backing to get off the ground. That will not be easy to find when you are just starring out. If you work for a large organisation and have a well established track record, it will be easier, but there is always going to be an element of risk in making entertainment films made for public showing. When you start your career you may find it easier to consider some of the other things films can do, which you may also have included on your list. Films can educate and train. Those words may not immediately set you alight, especially if you have recently been in a school and college for what you may think was far too long. For a film maker they are words which are too important to ignore. I bought two large family houses and started what became a multi national company on the profits from two training films I had made. In a moment I will explain how that happened and what you need to do in case you are interested in following a similar course. Before I do that, let's check some of the other headings you may have on your list. Does it include public relations? Films can present an image of a product, a service or an organisation and persuade audiences to adopt a particular point of view. They can be encouraged to like or dislike, reject or buy, visit or ignore, believe or overlook, what your films can show. As a film Producer, you will have an armoury of techniques which you can can employ to get your messages across.

On your list you should also have acknowledged the fact that films can sell. Every day people buy things they have possibly been introduced to to by films and television programmes. Perhaps it is a product or a service, or maybe it's a holiday. The variety of the things films can sell is huge and the opportunities that affords you as a film maker should not be ignored. Films are international. You can shoot in one language and show your end product in many more. Making your film is the first challenge. Targeting the right audience in the right way is crucial if you and your sponsor are going to benefit. Here too there are mistakes I can help you to avoid.

When you have completed your first production you will need to launch it, so people know it is there and you will need to distribute it so it reaches the right audience in the most cost effective way. To do all these things you may need to set up a business. You may start, as I did with a portable typewriter. You of course will now have a laptop computer, but the steps you will need to take if you are going to succeed, and the pitfalls you will need to avoid, are basically the same.

So when you start out, how do you let the people you will need know you are around? When I left the BBC and decided to set up and produce films with a handful of colleagues, we wondered how to get ourselves known. We no longer worked for a national television network. We were nobodies from nowhere, and we had to start from scratch. We needed to let people know we were around. I was young and knew nothing about how to start or run a business. We wanted to contact businessmen who might help us to raise cash and sponsor our films. I was so naïve I thought all businessmen would read the London *Financial Times.* At minimal cost which was far more than we could afford, I arranged to put a small advertisement on an inside page. It gave the name we had decided to use and proclaimed that we produced films for industry and television. The ad duly appeared and we all bought a copy but I don't think anyone else can have done. Weeks later we did receive one enquiry. It was from a company which made plastic sheet film for roofing.

They had seen our advertisement and wondered if they could supply us with their plastic film! It was clear that we were going to have to learn how to start and run our business the hard way!

Before we could start trading we needed to decide what sort of films we were going to make.When we had made that decision we needed to work out how we were going to operate. In the BBC we only had to pick up a phone to get anything any Producer could ever want. Now we were "outside". We were nobodies with nothing and, at first, we did not know where to start. As far as film making was concerned we had been properly trained. I had spent three years learning the basics, as I have already explained. One of my new colleagues had been on the same course. He was one of the best best lighting Cameramen I have ever known. The third member of our initial team was interested in sound. When it came to doing what we were hoping to make a living from, we thought we should at least stand a chance. As far as business matters were concerned, we knew less than nothing. So how were we going to find any customers and persuade them to do business with us? Democracy and a few pints in our local pub, enabled us to reach our first boardroom decision. We needed a shop window. As we were planning to make films which we wanted sponsors to finance we needed to be able to shown them what they would get for their money. Who could we find to back our first sponsored film?

We wrote to every potential sponsor we could think of, and got lots of letters back. They all said they were not interested in making films or they were every happy with their present suppliers. It was clear we had to produce something we could show. With that in mind we started to look around for people who, as an act of kindness or desperation, might give us a chance.

At that time, at weekends I used to drive down to Brighton where my parents had been living since my father had retired. One weekend I decided to take them for a picnic in the country.

We set out towards Eastbourne along quiet country roads. In a small village we came across a roadside shop. There was a sign outside advertising locally produced country wines. We decided to investigate. In what had once been a country house, until half of it had been destroyed in a fire, the owner of the business and his nephew had started making cider. They were a splendid team whose hobbies I later discovered were collecting vintage fire engines and lawnmowers! They had great plans for the future but at that stage not a lot of cash.

They had a small vineyard and their aim was to see it expand and become Britain's leading producer of of top quality wines. In the interim they had started by making cider from local apples and had built up a good business. They called their cider Merrydown-wine of Sussex, because the tax on cider was then excessive. Their products were good. They were nice people and they knew what they were doing and I felt sure it was only a matter of time before their business took off. The only thing they lacked and clearly needed, as I was quick to point out, was their own promotional film!

We made M*ERRYDOWN - WINE OF SUSSE*X in three weeks. It was shot with basic equipment in the partially burned out building which housed their the company's very short bottling line, and at a small number of other locations nearby. Their products were good and our film made all the points they wanted to get across. I edited it and wrote a commentary. My next job was to find the right person to read it on the finished film. I wanted to get a well known name because I knew that would help Merrydown to sell their products. Most big names wanted big money even then, so I had to look around. Working at the BBC I had got to know quite a lot of actors and actresses and wondered who I could approach and ask if they would do the job. As you will discover when you start making films, voice over commentaries require special skills. I have worked with a number of actors who are brilliant on screen but, when their voices are heard out of view, they do not have the same authority. The quality of the voice may not be right. It may not be strong enough to stand out over music and sound effects. I have also worked with a lot of excellent artistes who specialize in voice over work and are rarely seen in vision. For our Merrydown film I decided to approach a man who worked for BBC radio but had not yet been seen on television. He introduced and anchored a prestige early morning programme which had then just begun. It was and still is called *TODAY*, and it's first anchorman was Jack De Manio.

Jack had started his broadcasting career as an Announcer on what was then known as the BBC Home Service. He was was seconded to the Overseas Service to report on a Royal visit to Nigeria. He was supposed to read out the programme title when it began and say "Welcome to the land of the Niger." Unfortunately in the heat of the moment on a live broadcast, he managed to put an extra "G" in an inappropriate place, which caused uproar even then!

When I met him ten years later he was a respected and cherished household name, with a reputation for always getting his time checks wrong. He agreed to read my commentary and was a delight to work with. That film, which was lost for many years has recently been found and digitally restored, It is, of course, old fashioned by today's standards but it stands up reasonably well as is an interesting relic from interesting times. It served Merrydown very well indeed. It also proved to be a good shop window to encourage sponsors to spend their money with us.

Our Merrydown venture was in many ways a dual purpose film. Normally I am totally against trying to do two different jobs in one film. If a sponsor asks us to make a promotional film which can also be used for staff training I always say "No." The two aims are fundamentally different and, if a film is to succeed it must have one clear goal. Either it sets out to sell a product, a service or something else. Or it aims to train the staff who will provide what is being sold. Merrydown did serve two purposes but that was not its original intention.

ON LOCATION THIS WEEK

It sold the company's products very well indeed. It also promoted a positive image of a brand which at that time to most people was entirely new. Its success prompted a number of other much larger organisations with in similar businesses to approach us to ask if we would like to work for them.

The nice thing about repeat business, or business which comes to you on the recommendation of those you have worked for before, is that it costs you nothing. I have been lucky throughout my career. Apart from the Financial Times advertisement I mentioned earlier, which appeared when we first started, we have only advertised the availability of copies of films we have completed. Production contracts have come to us as a result of people seeing our films or talking to the customers we made them for. After Merrydown I was approached by one of Britain's biggest breweries which was about to get even bigger than it had ever been. In 1971 Whitbread was producing over seven million hectolitres of beer a year. When we first heard from them, they were finalising a marketing agreement with one of the biggest continental names in beer - a family-owned company controlled and run by one man. - Gerald A Heineken. The Heineken name was then almost unknown in Britain. Whitbread and their public relations advisers wanted to do something about that and asked me if we would like to get involved.

Their main goal was public relations. People who knew the right names bought the right beer - that was the main thought behind their the brief they gave us. Now if you are going to set up in film production today, the lessons we learned working for them are just as valid now. I will briefly explain what they wanted to achieve, how we went about it and what that involved.

To get the Heineken name in front of as many people as possible, the two companies had agreed to sponsor a number of sporting events. They wanted to appeal to the top end of the beer market and planned to sponsor a Dunkirk style flotilla of small boats to race from Ramsgate in Kent to Amsterdam in Holland.

The boats would all be gin palaces afloat and no expense would be spared in staging the event. They also also decided to build what would be the world's largest hot air balloon. It would to be called the Gerald A Heineken. Unlike most balloons, which carried up to half a dozen people, the Heineken would carry 30 passengers and crew. We were invited to quote for making films about of both these events, which would take place in the course of a year.

The cross channel boat race proved to be the hardest to film. To cover something like that properly you need quite a lot of cameras. We had four. One was to travel on one of the boats. Two others would be with me in Amsterdam to shoot everything as it happened when the boats arrived. I heard Heineken were going to charter a small plane to fly above the convoy as it entered Amsterdam and I arranged to put a Cameraman aboard.

If you are ever asked to film a similar event, you will find costing what you have to do is not an easy task. If one of your Cameramen is travelling in a million pound yacht, owned by one of the competitors, you will also need to add a significant sum for bottles of gin! When the flotilla was due to arrive I positioned two cameras near the main harbour building, which is in the centre of town next to Amsterdam station. I knew all the boats would have to pass that point. I planned to have my third camera with me on the roof of the building.

From there I would be able to speak by radio to all my crews, including the fifth Cameraman who was going to be flying overhead in the specially chartered aircraft. The owners of the plane had agreed to allow us to open a door in the side of the fuselage and tie it back so our Cameraman could get a clear view of what was happening down below.

As the flotilla sailed into Amsterdam we shot as many shots as we could from different angles. It was a lovely clear day and everything looked wonderful. Our carefully laid plans were working exactly as we had hoped. At just the right moment our chartered aircraft appeared on the horizon and flew above the boats towards us. As it passed above the boat which was leading the procession, I saw a bright flash as if a silver object had just caught the sun. At exactly that point the aircraft turned, banked steeply and flew away. I thought the plane was being repositioned to get a better shot but then a nightmarish thought crossed my mind. Had my cameraman fallen out of the plane? It had happened in seconds but my worries went on. I glanced round again. Everything looked as it had before before. The boats continued to sail into the harbour in an orderly way. Only one thing was missing. There was no aircraft to be seen. On my radio I tried to call the Cameraman who was aboard. There was no response. The line had gone dead.

The hours that followed were among the longest in my life. The boats entered harbour and we filmed everything which took place. There was still no word about the plane and, as time passed, I began to think I was imagining a problem which did not exist. Everything looked so peaceful and normal. It was late that evening, when a clearly shaken Cameraman returned to our hotel that I heard what had happened. A panel from the aircraft door, which had been opened and pinned back, had broken loose and fallen into the harbour. Miraculously it did not do any damage but it set off an alarm. The Pilot had reacted immediately, turned and headed for the nearest airport where he made a safe emergency landing. When the aircraft was checked there was no damage and everyone involved was safe and accounted for. The Cameraman was shaken but, in the middle of the crisis he had kept his camera running and got an excellent shot which we included in our film. I don't think his wife was ever told how that shot was obtained!

At the start of that project we had taken out insurance for all the crews involved in case anything went awry and, as you have just heard, it was just as well we did. Some film companies tend to dismiss insurance as just another overhead. They should consider what they might have to face. I learned that lesson when I was working for the BBC. On one occasion we had to shoot some scenes on Concorde, which at that time was the world's newest and most expensive aircraft. We were warned in advance that we would need to tread with extreme care as we were being insured for a million pounds a day. It all seemed a bit far fetched at the time as, when we were shooting, the aircraft was on the ground outside terminal three. Our shots simply showed the crew serving a meal to passengers, who on this occasion were airline staff who had been suitably disguised. When the film was edited we added clouds outside and suitable sound effects to make it look and sound as if Concorde was in the air. Only those who were there at the time ever knew what happened, but from that day on I made a mental note to check that anyone I filmed was properly insured just in case!

I was to fly in Concorde again later on. On that occasion I was travelling as a fare paying passenger on an Air France Concorde from Paris to New York. It was a memorable flight in every way. Concorde was small but it did not feel cramped. It flew way above the highest clouds at supersonic speeds. Air France served a memorable lunch shortly after we took off from Orly airport at 11am Paris time. We landed in NewYork at 11am New York time after five hours in the air. Very few Concordes were ever made. British Airways had a few and Air France had five. A few months after I had made my New York flight one of the Air France planes crashed shortly after taking off from Orly. There were no survivors. It was the same flight I had caught a few months earlier and I have often wondered if it was the same aircraft. I am not sure if I really want to know.

One of the great joys of making films for a living is the variety of different experiences you will have making the productions you decide to take on. You should be able to work on a wide range of different subjects, perhaps shooting them in different countries. You will meet and work for and with people with very different views. I have just told you about one of our public relations films. It set out to build an image of a company and to sell their products - In that case beer. The success of that film brought us business from other sponsors and, if I tell you about some of them and what they wanted us to do you will see how diverse your life can be.

Following our Heineken success we were approached by a large British company which had interests in a number of different services and products. Then it was British owned and run. Today some of its interests have been sold off and a large part of the group we were originally asked to work for is now American owned. The company that approached us was P & O., which had started life as the Peninsular and Oriental shipping company and then invested in other things. Their main business was operating cruise and cargo ships around the world. When we first got involved they had just diversified into property development and it was that side of the business which had encouraged them to approach us. The company had recently been granted planning permission to develop a huge and very prestigious London riverside site. It wasn't very prestigious when we first saw it. Though its potential was obvious, for several years it had been used as a dumping ground for hundreds of wrecked cars. P and O had spotted an opportunity, realised the site's true potential and fought for several years to get planning permission which had finally been granted. They planned to build a massive riverside development which they intended to call Chelsea Harbour. There would be flats, houses and a 5 star hotel on a prime site on the Thames, a few minutes stroll from Battersea Bridge. The fashionable Kings Road and Chelsea's main shopping areas were just minutes away. It was to be a landmark development in every sense and P & O were keen to record its progress and get as much publicity as they could for what was being done. That, as you will have guessed, is where we came in!

Our initial contract was to film the clearing of the site. It was going to be a difficult site to work on. The Thames ran down one side and one of London's busiest roads down another. London Underground had railway tracks running across the site and a main railway line ran through another area. Lots Road Power Station, which generated power for much of the London underground network, was yards away and many of the services supplying that part of London ran either under the site or nearby.

The project Manager - John Anderson who was an immensely able man, had estimated that the project would take around three years to complete. Work began the day after planning permission had been granted and we started to film on the same day. For two years we filmed everything that moved. We watched as buildings went up at an astonishing rate. As the original Chelsea harbour basin, which had been silted up for years, was dredged out and turned into a new Chelsea Harbour we were there. When one of London's busiest railway lines had to be moved, and a bridge it was carried on demolished and replaced in one weekend, we filmed it as it happened. By the time the first apartments were ready for sale we had the basis of a first class film.

As work had progressed we prepared interim edited versions of our footage to keep everyone informed. They showed what was happening and the extraordinary speed at which the work was being done. Those interim films helped P & O to keep people who needed to be kept in the know informed about what was going on. Our film, though by no means completed, was already earning its keep. When the first phase of the project was completed, we were asked to make a marketing film to help to sell what had been done and bring in money to finance the next stage. That film proved to be a sound investment from our sponsor's point of view. I remember a very senior P and O Manager telling me that he had been woken up at a very early hour one morning by a wealthy American lady who insisted on speaking to him. She had just seen our film on a P and O ship on which was cruising, and wanted to buy a London home at Chelsea Harbour! By the time we completed our contract, Chelsea Harbour was up and running. Today the film has been digitally restored and is many peoples' prize possession. A unique record of the great success of a well organised company, and the arrival of a new landmark on London's skyline.

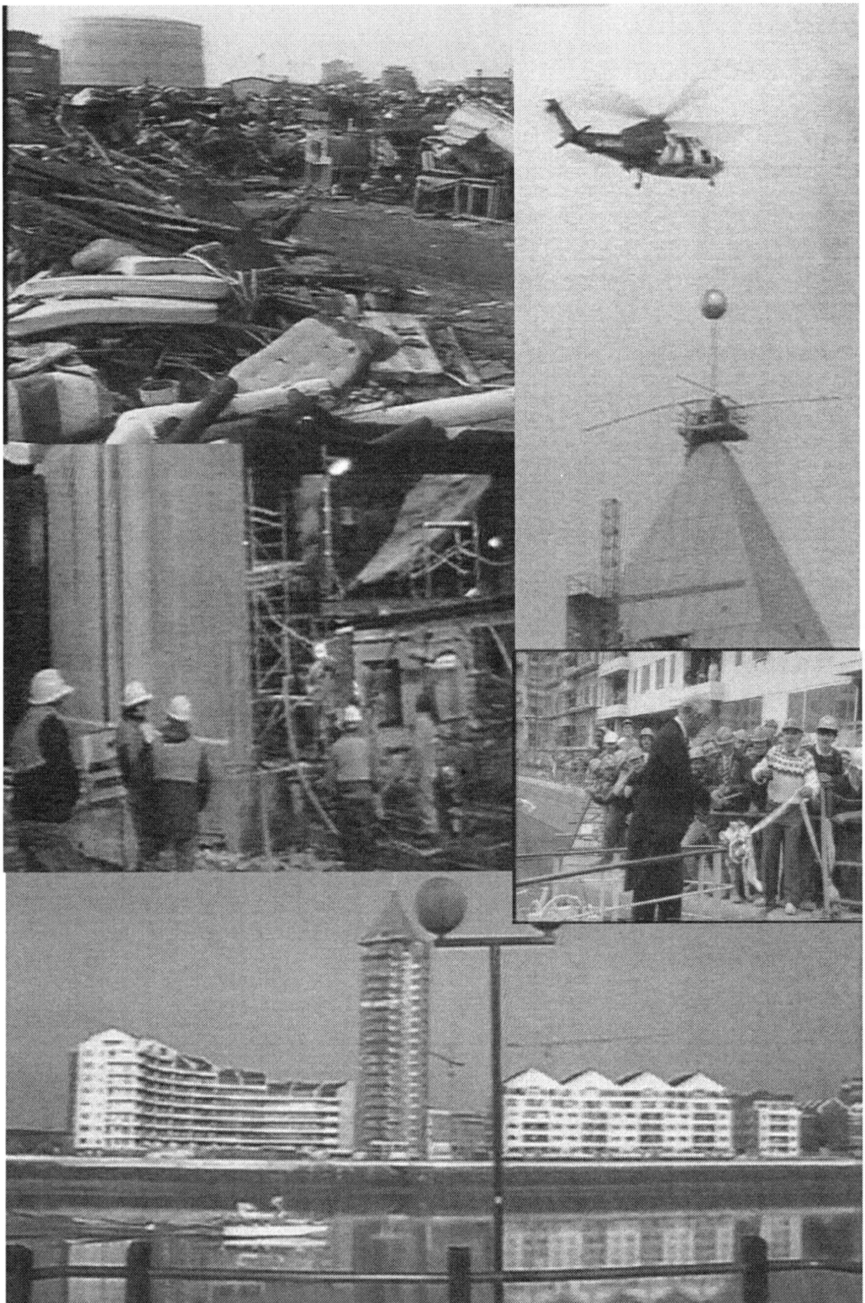

If you decide to spend your life making films, you will find that recording projects like the one I have just mentioned can help you to build your business. Later in these pages I will give you some more examples of the sort of people who you can persuade to spend their money with you and what you can do for them. From Chelsea we went abroad for our next major project. We won a contract in competition with a lot of much larger well established companies. It was a contract which was far larger than we had ever envisaged It took two years to complete, because we were doing other jobs in between, and it was shot entirely overseas. Our client on this occasion was not a commercial company. It was a government and, as that is another market you may wish to explore, I will explain what it involved and how we won and carried out first overseas contract.

When Chelsea Harbour was becoming the fashionable place to be, I was approached by a representative of the Saudi Arabian Government. Their London embassy was in Notting Hill, not far from Chelsea, and they had heard about our activities there. As a new organisation, with limited resources and relatively little experience, I was surprised they had come to us. I was also delighted to have a chance to quote for what sounded like quite a big job in a part of the world I would otherwise have been unlikely to see. Dealing with Saudi Arabia, as I was soon to learn, is unlike dealing with almost any other country. The Kingdom of Saudi Arabia is not sort of cash. Oil revenues have made it rich. If you were born in the Kingdom you do not have to work to earn a living. You will be well looked after. The country consists of a few modern commercial centres, religious shrines and miles of desert where oil is produced. In the two years I worked in the country I began to understand and like the Saudi people. Anyone working there will need patience and understanding. Their ways of doing things are not as they are in the west, but they are honest and reliable and we had no problem establishing a good working relationship with them from day one. On his first approach to me, the Saudi Ambassador's Representative in London told me they were preparing to "build "a new city" and wanted to tell the story of the project on

Saudi television and around the world. They wanted a film produced simultaneously in Arabic and English and had invited six well established companies in major countries outside the Arab world to quote for doing the job.

They came to us because they knew what we had done at Chelsea, just up the road. As you will discover if you are asked to undertake any large project, preparing a quotation is not a easy job. The "city" they were planning to build turned out to be a massive water treatment plant. It would be surrounded by new houses and industrial buildings so what had been a desert would become a place where people could live. That was easy to understand but, when we looked at a map we found the proposed site was 230 miles from the nearest town. The only way of getting there was to drive, in a suitably equipped 4 wheel drive vehicle, across 230 miles of desert. And all this took place years before satellite navigation and mobile phones had been invented.

In preparing our quotation I had worked out what I thought it would cost to make the film in the UK. I allowed for all the things I allow for when I do any quote. The equipment we would need. The number of people who would be required to shoot, edit and record, and the time for which each person would need to be involved. I calculated the amount of film I estimated we needed to shoot and, in those days, added the cost of processing that film and making copies in a film laboratory. I allowed for six weeks editing in a fully equipped cutting room in the UK. To those basic costs I added the additional cost of translating the final script into Arabic and recording both an English and an Arabic version, with suitable fees for the artistes who would be involved. Finally I added a contingency fee - 20 percent of my estimated cost of production. I then completed my figures by adding a profit margin for the amount we wanted to make on the deal. What I deliberately did not include was any figure for travel, and living expenses incurred in getting from our UK base to and from any of the locations at which we must film, or while we were working there.

We thought we could cover what we had to show in three visits of two weeks each while the construction work was going in.

Two months later we heard that we had been chosen to do the job and I set off to fly to Jeddah and sign a contract. I arrived on one of the Saudi national airline's latest aircraft - a brand new Boeing 747. As we taxied towards the terminal building I got up and prepared to leave. The aircraft stopped and a gangway was lowered front of the plane. After a long delay a handful of people started to get off. I moved towards the exit but before I could get anywhere near it the aircraft moved on. There were now quite a lot of people waiting to get off but the aircraft continued on its course. A Steward, who saw we were worried, started to reassure us. "Don't worry" he said. We will be stopping in a moment. "That was the Royal Terminal, where only members of the Royal Family and their guests are allowed to get off". His explanation posed more questions than it answered. Had the people I had seen alighting been the King with members of his family? It was two days later that I learned out what I had seen. I had witnessed the arrival of a visiting cricket team who had been invited to play against a royal team. Their arrival had delayed our flight by over an hour and God knows what it had cost in aircraft fuel, but that did not matter. No one seemed to care! When we started to shoot, every three months we flew out from London. We caught a morning flight which arrived in Saudi as the end of the day. We then drove all night across the desert. It was cooler at that time and our four wheel drive Toyota, with five people and thirteen cases of camera equipment on board, somehow managed to cope. Our driver was Turkish. As he did not speak English and we knew no Turkish we got on surprisingly well. Our journeys were interrupted by the odd sandstorm but they generally passed more smoothly that we had any right to expect. Our main worry was that, charging across the desert at the dead of night, we would collide with one of the stray camels which make it their home. They didn't wear

Lights! We had been told that, if we did hit one, we would probably die before we knew what had happened, and the many wrecked vehicles we passed on our way was a constant reminder of what was at stake.

When our film was finished and the "city" built, our client arranged a huge party. It was held in in very elaborate tents with the finest carpets rolled out to cover the desert sand. The local Sheikh and a Royal Prince were the Guests of Honour and no expense was spared. It was a nice end to what had been a very enjoyable commission. Our film was completed on schedule and within our predicted budget. I think the people who asked us to make it were happy because a few months later they asked us to make another. This time they were going to build "the word's most modern hospital". We submitted our quote and hoped we would be able to deliver what our customer wanted again.

In between our Saudi visits in the two years that film took to complete, we managed to make a number of other films in the UK and in other parts of Europe They were all quite successful but some were more enjoyable than others to make. One of the most trying was a sales promotional film we made for the British subsidiary of a large French owned travel company. They specialised in up market holidays at a number of specially built seaside locations in smart parts of Europe. Their holidays were fine. We had no problem making them look very good indeed. Our main concern was the liaison man our sponsor had appointed to monitor our work. He was English, and he knew everything about everything, at least he thought he did. As a liaison man he was a complete disaster because he could upset anyone from a hundred yards away. He even managed to upset us, and that is an almost impossible task. He, of course, thought he knew all about making films and never lost a chance to tell us what we should be doing and what we were doing wrong. When you are filming in a very hot climate for three weeks and working twelve hours a day that kind of help is not very welcome. He thought he was Steven Spielberg and pursued us everywhere. We eventually managed to lose him when we discovered he rather like Schnapps. A couple of bottles left outside his room after a day filming usually meant he did not emerge too early next day. He eventually got the point and decided it was easier for him to stay put and let us get on with the job. Our last problem with him came when our film had been edited and we were about to record the final commentary. I had arranged for one of the best voice over artistes (Paul Vaughan, who had worked with me on the BBC *Horizon* programme) to record the English version, and a well French broadcaster to record in French. Our client did everything he could to to stop us. It was, as he constantly reminded us, his film. Our sponsor had told him to make sure it was alright and it was his job to ensure it sounded right on the finished film. The only way he could be sure that would happen was to read it himself. My attempts to persuade him that others might perhaps have a different point of view fell on deaf ears. In a last desperate move, I arranged to take him and our edited film to the recording studio we planned to use. I showed him what we were going to do and then asked him to sit down and read the commentary for us. When his cue light came on, he began to read and we started to record. We did half the first paragraph a dozen times and then, at last, he got the point and gave up. He sulked for the rest of the day but we knew we had won and the film we had worked so hard to perfect had been saved. It went on to do much better than we had ever thought it would. It also brought us a lot of new business from clients we might otherwise never have met. We began to realise just how big the travel films market can be if it is properly exploited. I am sure you have seen promotional films and television programmes which have made you wish you were there - on holiday in the place or places featured. I will bet you never thought about the people who made those films. If you care to spend a few minutes doing so, you may find another key to a successful career. Let me make one point straight away. Making films about holidays is very hard work. One of the things which annoyed me when we were asked to make a film on a holiday or travel subject was the attitude our friends seemed to adopt. They always thought that we we would be lying in the sun and sipping drinks in exotic places. They could not have been more wrong. As the Producer of a film someone else is paying you to make, your job is to do what that sponsor requires. Most sponsors do know what they want, but not all. If they are sensible they also welcome other peoples ideas as to how their aims can best be put across. If they are unwise, they may try and do your job for you, like our friend with the schnapps. Or they may expect you to do what they think you do quite well, 24 hours a day. They may sometimes have the wrong objectives. Films for companies selling cruises were prone to that until a few years ago, and some still are. They wanted to project an image of well equipped ships, full of happy people having a very good time. In reality a lot of them were running very old ships which catered for people who were often as old, or considerably older, than the vessels they were travelling in. Fortunately most of those companies have either gone out of business or got the message.

As a result, making films promoting holidays is now easier, but but it is never a holiday! If you are going to do it properly it is always hard work but it can be very rewarding from every point of view. If I give you a few examples of what we encountered, it may help to give you ideas for jobs you might like to do.

One of the most successful and enjoyable films we made was a film on the maiden voyage of P& O's cruise ship *ORIANA*. Before I tell you what that involved,you may care to *stop reading for a moment and think what you would have done if* **you** *had been asked to make that film.*

MAIDEN VOYAGE ON ORIANA

Our brief was simple. ORIANA was the newest and, at that time the largest, ship in the P & O fleet. It had been built at enormous cost to very high standards and had been given a lot of publicity in the press. Now P & O wanted it to start making money and that was where we came in. So, how are **you** going to tackle a subject like that and what do you think making your film is going to involve you in? Having made a number of films on various ships over the years, I can tell you a few things you will not find in the brochures of the company you are being paid to promote. The first is that, as a film crew, you will be working while everyone else is lounging around. You will inevitably encounter people who don't want to be filmed. They may be there with other people's husbands or wives, or perhaps they want to draw attention to themselves and the only way they can do that is to create a fuss. Most people are usually happy to be involved, if they are asked politely if they would mind being filmed. A few minutes explaining what you are doing and how you would like them to be involved, can save a lot if heartache. You will also learn that ships are not always as stable as they look in cruise brochures. I have had to film in a force 9 gales, when most of the passengers and sometimes crew are feeling so ill they don't want to get up. It is not easy making things look attractive on days like that. You however will be working to a budget and a day of filming lost is going to put your schedule out of gear. If you have enough members of your crew who are fit enough to carry on, you may be able to shoot something which carries on regardless of what is happening outside. We shot scenes in an engine room, where nothing much changes, and close ups of artworks in other areas, on one of our roughest trips. Those shots were later cut together with shots of the same areas being used when conditions were calmer. On Oriana we never had that problem. On her maiden voyage the seas were calm and on subsequent occasions when we returned to shoot more films on the ship, she proved to be a true and gentle lady of the seas. So, how are **you** going to make *your* maiden voyage film?

As a film Producer you have plenty of possibilities you can explore. You must decide how you are going to present your film to the audiences your sponsor wants to reach. In deciding how to do that, there are two key words you must never forget. *Aims and Audience.* They have to be brought together in a way which will make both parties happy with your end result.

You will find your objective is easier to achieve if you remember that, if audiences are to get pleasure from what they are shown they need to be entertained,They also generally like to learn something and be kept informed. That doesn't mean your film has to contain a laugh a minute or be an endless list of boring facts. They may or may not be interested to know how many bottles of champagne are consumed on an average cruise but facts like that should be used sparingly and inserted at appropriate points and not used throughout like a sales catalogue.

Another common pitfall, which inexperienced film makers often fall into, is a soundtrack which tells audiences what they can already see for themselves. Films are made up to two key elements, Sounds and pictures. If your film is going to work,you need to use both elements as creatively as possible. Every shot needs to tell a story or make a point. A commentary, which lists the sales points your sponsor wants to makes from beginning to end, will just encourage people to switch off or not believe anything they are being told. Your soundtrack will need to contain more than a commentary. If the pictures you shoot are to come to life, you need good sound effects and music at strategic points to avoid what is generally referred to as wall to wall words.

If you have any doubts about the importance of taking trouble with your soundtrack, next time you watch a television documentary, turn off the sound and watch it for a few minutes. The longer you watch the more you can learn. Without music and / or sound effects pictures lack life. Films seem slower and probably less interesting. Used sparingly and creatively, sound effects and music can bring your film to life.

A lazy film maker will shoot everything without sound and add music, and probably little else, in the dubbing theatre at a later stage. That is acceptable if the music is right for the scenes and it is used in the correct way. It is better if music can be recorded earlier and pictures then edited so they can be made to work with the soundtrack in the most effective manner. If you have a large enough budget you may be able to afford to have music specially composed for your film. That will generally be done when editing has been completed or is well underway A video copy of your edited version can give your Composer an idea of the content and length of the shots his or her music has to cover.

Alternatively you can use what is known as mood music. That is the name given to commercially published recorded music which has been written specially for use on stage and in films. As a film Producer you will be asked to pay a royalty for any music you decide to use. That sum is normally calculated on the time your music is being heard and the type film it is being used on. If you are using three minutes of mood music in an educational film which is only going to be used in schools, it will cost you much less than it will if it is going to be transmitted by television networks around the world.

Our *ORIANA* film took six weeks to complete. We filmed on board for two weeks. We then shot additional footage at some of the ports at which she had visited and edited the footage in our cutting rooms.

The film included a commentary written and recorded in the penultimate stage. As you will realise if you are asked to make a film, as a film Producer you can present the story you have to tell in many different ways. The same applies to film commentaries. They can be written in the the first or the third person, or any other way to suit the character who audiences are

For example, our maiden voyage film commentary could have been written for an impersonal Narrator who spoke as a cruise company spokesman. *"Oriana cost over two million pounds to build and the work took two years to complete"* …. etc etc. Alternatively it could have been personalised, as if the words were being spoken by the ship's Captain or one of his officers. *"On our ships we try to provide everything anyone could want"*… etc etc.. Using that kind of approach will allow you to write in a more personal way, which audiences are a more likely to appreciate and accept. Or you could have written it so it appeared to be the voice of a passenger, who had experienced what we had decided to show…. "So what was it like on Britain's newest cruise ship? That is what we were able to find out On a maiden voyage things don't always go according to plan but"… etc etc…. That was the course I decided to adopt and it worked very well.

I have always tried to avoid boring commentaries for the same reasons I try to avoid people standing still and talking to camera. Unless they have exceptional personalities, they are unlikely to be interesting to listen to or to watch for shot after shot.

Our first *ORIANA* film was a great success and we later returned to make two more films. Like Oriana herself, it has now been around for some time but it has recently been digitally restored and is now available on DVD. At the end of this book you will find details of how it and some of the other films mentioned in the text can be obtained.

If you think you would like to earn a living making films yourself, later in this book you will find a test exercise which is designed to help you find out if you are likely to be a success or not. Many people think they want to work in films but, as I have already mentioned, they do not always think about their aims enough before they start out. Research has shown that the average life of a new film company is three years. It is much the same for a lot of fledgling businesses in other areas but making films is often thought to be a glamorous occupation when in fact it is a business and it has to pay its way. Most new companies fail because they are under capitalised or they are aiming for the wrong goals. As many do not survive more than three years, and we have been making films profitably for 37, we like to believe that somehow, somewhere, we may be doing something right!

When **you** are a success, and if you heed the warnings contained in this book I see no reason why you should not be, you will find potential new customers will often come to you. That will save you the cost of advertising your services . Most of our business now comes from people who have liked productions we have made or have been put in touch with us by the people we have made films for.

The *Oriana* films produced a flood of new business and introduced us to countries and subjects we had never considered or explored. In case you want to cash in on opportunities we missed, I will briefly tell you about a few of the films we made as a result of those enquiries. Our first enquiry came from just across he sea. None of us had ever thought about or visited the Channel Islands but we ere soon to find out what we had missed

The Channel Islands are just a short flight or ferry crossing from England's south coast but for all we knew then it could have been a million miles away. We knew nothing about Guernsey but they had heard about us and apparently been told we made "quite nice films." That lead to our being approached by the island's Tourist Board. They telephoned me and asked if they could come and see us when they were next in London to discuss a project they were thinking about. We carried out a few checks and discovered that in the past they had made some films with other companies but to us that was nothing new. On the appointed day half a dozen members of their committee arrived as we had arranged. We welcomed them with coffee and showed them a couple of films. By then it was lunch time and we thought we should offer our guests a drink or invite them to lunch which we then did. We had completed a very useful meeting and had got on well and were looking forward to entertaining a group of people we really liked but they were adamant.

They could not stay as they had another meeting to go on to. They said they liked what they had seen and would be in touch. We were sad about that because we thought we had lost a potentially interesting film and people we would have enjoyed working with.

About a month later we heard what had happened. The leader of the team who had visited us told me they had been very impressed by what they had heard and seen. They wanted to stay for the hospitality we had offered but they had been told that we were all teetotal and the prospect of a day in London at lunch time, with a group of teetotalers did not appeal so they went elsewhere! When they discovered that their informant had taken them for a ride, and the reports they had heard could not be further from the truth, we got the job and began a great working partnership which lasted for many years. Guernsey has been one of my favourite holiday destinations ever since. We made a number of films about the three islands which make up what is known as the Bailiwick of Guernsey. Guernsey itself, and the other islands in the group - Alderney, Herm and Sark, are delightfully different and have much to offer. We made a several tourist films and the award winning *ECHOES OF THE PAST* which has recently been digitally restored and is now available on DVD. You will find further details at the end of this book.

Echoes of the Past

The history of the Bailiwick of GUERNSEY

From the Channel Islands our next commission was to take us much further from home to work for a very different client. Once again we would be working for a government and not for a commercial concern. Our last governmental client had been Saudi Arabia - one of the the richest countries in the world. Our next potential client was one of the poorest. Sri Lanka, which for many years was known as Ceylon. The main income for this idyllic island in the Indian ocean comes from tourism. In an attempt to boost trade, they had decided to sponsor two tourist films. One would be aimed at audiences of travel agents. The other would target their customers. Though Sri Lanka is what is generally described as a third world country, it is used to dealing with big international concerns. When they decided they wanted to make a film, they approached a host of well established companies in seven major countries. All received the same brief. To win a contract everyone knew that, whatever they offered to do, would have to be made at what our potential sponsor would consider to be a reasonable price. As one of the smallest and newest companies invited to quote, we did not think we stood much chance, but it was a job we knew we could do well. Though Sri Lanka is completely different to Guernsey, it is also a small island. The people it attracts are the sort of customers our films had appealed to before. The island has wonderful climate, with summer weather almost all year round. It is easy to reach. It is served by many international airlines and, as a low cost destination,visitors can usually get good value for their money. Those were some of the points we had to get across and I spent two weeks finding out about Sri Lanka and preparing our quotation. When it had been submitted we heard nothing for two months and assumed our hard work had ended in a bin but we were wrong. It had not. The Tourist Board's representative in London eventually telephoned me to explain that we had been short listed and they would like me to travel at their expense to Colombo to discuss what could be done. As a result of those discussions we won the contract we had hoped for, and produced two of the most enjoyable and successful films I have ever had the pleasure of working on.

If you should find yourself quoting to win a contract like that, what do you need to consider and do to have a a chance of winning? You have been told in the brief what your sponsor wants to achieve. Your first job is to decide what scenes you are going to need to show and what pictures and sounds you will need to bring that about. You can then plan where those shots need to be shot from and that will help you to asses your costs. You can calculate how much time you will need and how many minutes of tape or film you are likely to require. Getting to and from each location and the time you will stay there needs to be worked out too in some detail if you don't want to end up losing money. Will you need any overnight stays or have to pay living costs as well as accommodation? When you are shooting, will you be able to shoot by available light or will portable lighting or generators be required? What sounds do you need to capture and what are you going to record them on? Are you going to shoot them at the same time as your pictures, and will they be shot synchronised to your film or recorded independently at the same time or earlier or later? These may not sound like major points but they can have a huge bearing in what your film will cost to make. Time is money in film making, just as it is in any other business and it is important to get your estimates right. If you are shooting using hired in cameras, sound or any other equipment, the daily cost per item will need to be added in. You can hire most professional cameras, recorders and lots of other gear on a daily,weekly or longer term basis. If you are using equipment you own, you should allow a percentage of the cost of replacing it on a regular basis so it does not wear out or become out of date. When you come to prepare your final soundtrack, if you are going to use commercially available mood music, you will need to work out an estimated cost for the amount of screen time you expect to use and the territories in which your finished film will be shown. If you are planning to arrange for music to be specially composed, the costs of composing and recording that will need to be added to your list of production costs. On top of all those costs need to add insurance and always allow a percentage for any any unexpected expenses you may incur. Ten percent of the overall cost you have calculated is a good place to start on that point. Finally you will need to add the cost of the technicians who will be involved at each stage of your production. The profit you hope to make must also be added before you submit your final quote.

If you take trouble considering each of the points I have mentioned, you are less likely to get a nasty shock if you quotation is accepted and you are then expected to deliver what your sponsor wants at the price you have quoted. If you are unable or unwilling to include travel and living expenses in your estimates, they can be excluded from your quote if you make that exclusion clear when you submit your quote. A sponsor may welcome that exclusion and be able to provide what is required at a lower price than you could arrange. In our Sri Lanka quote we excluded all travel and living cost. The Sri Lankan Government met all the travel and,living expenses for the crew throughout and also provided a Sri Lankan Air Force helicopter for two weeks for aerial shots and to help us reach less accessible points.

When it was completed the trade version of our film was used by travel agents in all Sri Lanka's key markets. The public version was released in a number of different languages and widely used around the world. It was selected for showing at the World Tourism Film Festival, which that year was held in New York and attracted entries from almost every country with a tourist industry. Since our film was made Sri Lanka has been involved in a civil war and had to cope with a hurricane and tsunami in which hundreds of people died. I am pleased to say that today it has largely recovered from those disasters and is once again a delightful place to enjoy a holiday. Though some things have inevitably changed, the friendliness of the Sri Lankan people and the sheer beauty of their island home is much as it a when we made our film. It has recently been digitally restored and is now available on DVD.

Photographed by
ALISTAIR CAMERON

Written & Directed by
JOHN BURDER

The films we made in Sri Lanka were essentially travel films but their main aim was of course to sell. In that instance our job was to sell the attractions of a country. As a film Producer you will find you can boost your business by helping to sell a wide variety of different things around the world. We have been asked to make films on some pretty odd subjects. Sludge, missile defence systems, rheumatoid arthritis and medical records, to name but a few. I think you will agree that they are not the first topics that come to mind when you are looking for a subject to make into an interesting and entertaining film, but that is what we were expected to do.

If you are going to be a successful film Producer you will need to be able to make dull subjects interesting to watch. I am not saying that a film on the management of sludge or medical records needs to be treated in a way that will make it top of the bill at the Odeon Leicester Square. That isn't your goal. What you will need to do is interest the audience your sponsor wants to reach and hold their attention from beginning to end. If you have original ideas that should help, but it does not always work out that way. Sponsors can sometimes be their own worst enemies if you only consider the products or services you have to promote, and forget that audiences need to be interested and entertained they may mentally switch off before your film is half way through. If you can capture their interest from the opening shots you stand a better change chance of getting your sponsor's message across. Alas there are sponsors who do not see things that way. They are few but they do exist and I have had the doubtful pleasure of working with for some in them in the course of my career and have lost several good opportunities as a result of their reluctance to consider any new ideas. Others have embraced original thoughts with enthusiasm and, in most case have been able to achieve all of their aims. One of the potentially dull subjects I was asked to film was a range of safety footwear. The company that approached me had never made a film before. They had considered it twice and on the second occasion has encouraged their Sales Manager, who was a keen amateur movie maker to do the job for them.

You will not be surprised if I reveal that the results were dire. That is a problem I have come across several times and a disease which can be difficult to cure. The footwear company was a large and successful business concern. Their products were good - among the best in the business .They had even managed to bring a touch of the fashion industry into the usually dull world of safety footwear. Every year they published a glossy new catalogue which listed their products and included full colour pictures of the most popular items. As a reference book it could not be bettered but it was not the sort of publication you would take with you to read on holiday or on a train. Their Publicity Manager thought their film should follow their catalogue line by line. I thought that be too boring for audiences to watch and suggested they might like to consider something a little more entertaining to get their message across. They reluctantly agreed to consider my proposal and I went off to try and dream up ideas, which could be used in conjunction with their catalogue, to deliver the boost in sales they wanted to see. At the time I had just finished working in mainstream television. I had been working on a project with the actor Kenneth Williams.

Kenny was at the peak of his career and working all hours. When I first met him he was doing three jobs at the same time. He was recording a radio programme - *JUST A MINUTE*- in the morning. When he finished that he was driven to Pinewood Studios to star in *CARRY ON CONSTABLE*. He ended each day at the Lyric Theatre where he was starring on stage in a review.

I got on well with Ken because he was wonderfully professional and expert at the things he enjoyed doing and did so well. I am often asked what he was like to work with. People assume that, because he made them laugh when he appeared on the screen, he was a bundle of fun all day long. In fact he was quite a serious man with strong views on a number of rather unlikely subjects. When we worked together he was always punctual or early.

He would turn up in a well cut tweed jacket and smartly pressed trousers and know everything about any script he had to perform. It was only when he stepped in front of a microphone or camera that he came totally to life. He would switch effortlessly from one voice to another and address a microphone as if it were another human being who had to be entertained. His complete mastery of radio technique taught me a lot. You are probably wondering what all this has to do with a film about protective footwear. As I mentioned earlier, in the course of my career I have always tried to avoid making films which are boring or fail to interest or entertain.

The brief we had been given for the proposed safety footwear film was a classic example of a subject which could easily be very tedious to watch. I thought it needed to be interpreted with a little imagination and not presented as a sales catalogue. After doing some research, I had an idea which I thought could be developed to get the points the company wanted to make across in a rather more interesting manner. In the film I wanted to make, every shot would be filmed at ground level. In stead of following a man or woman in every scene, we would just follow a pair of feet. The film's commentary would be written to give the feet a personality of their own. It would be the voice of the feet audiences would hear. They were not happy. Their owner took risks all day and expected them to go in dingy places narrowly avoiding crisis after crisis. Audiences would see some of those disasters as the voice explained how much nicer life would be if he could just get a nice pair of protective boots. I was confident we could develop that basic idea into quite a entertaining film and create a character audiences would would like and be able to identify with. It would also enable us to show a full range of our sponsor's products in an interesting way, and make all the sales points he wanted to impart without it sounding as if they were being read out of a sales catalogue.

I thought the idea would work but knew I needed to get other opinions before I offered it our potential sponsor. One of those whose opinion I sought was the actor who I hoped would provide the voice of the feet - the film's leading role - Kenneth Williams. With that in mind I sent him a script. Kenny liked it and said he would love to do it. He clearly really did like it, because he agreed to accept a much lower fee than he would normally get. After a lot of hard work, everything seemed to be going the right way and we were almost ready to go ahead.

Alas that film was never made. When I outlined my idea and presented the script Kenneth Williams had liked so much to our potential sponsor he nearly had a fit. He completely lost his cool and accused me of trying to send his products up and making a mockery of what they were trying to do. He had no sense of humour and very little imagination and was quite unable to understand what we had in mind. To support him he called in his Publicity Manager, who spent nine months each year preparing their sales catalogue and played bingo at weekends. Trying to persuade him to try something new really was like talking to a very thick brick wall. So that script was never produced, which I still think was a shame. Fortunately most if our clients were much more humane.

One of my favourite clients was a company which for years had produced a leading brand British tractors. David Brown Tractors was a well established Yorkshire firm. When we first started making films independently it had taken us two years to win our first contract from them. Their Publicity Manager was Donald Procter - a quiet and very knowledgeable Yorkshire man who was one of the best in the business. Month after month he had rejected our approaches and reminded me that they had worked with a Yorkshire based film company for many years. Fortunately Donald was prepared to listen to new ideas and in due course he agreed to meet me and see if there was anything we might do. We got on well and he liked our ideas and agreed to employ us to make their next film. It broke new ground and so well received that we continued to make their films for the next ten years. We also devised and and staged a live presentation for them in Monaco. Key customers and the Managers of their main suppliers and clients were flown to Monaco from all over Europe.

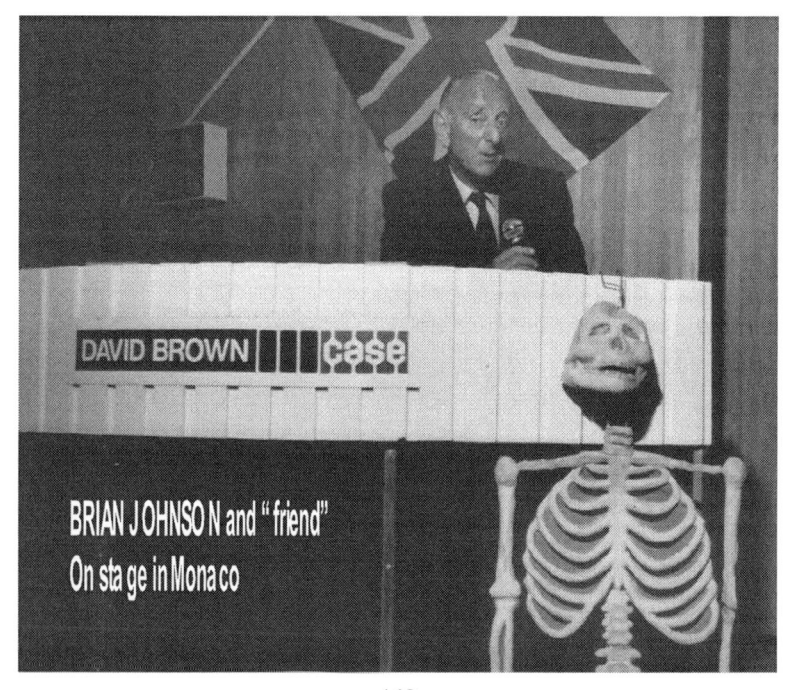

BRIAN JOHNSON and "friend"
On stage in Monaco

Years after that show took place, people still remind me of that day and say how much they enjoyed it. After that conference we were told in confidence that the company would shortly be introducing a new range of products. That was good news. It would mean they would need some new films, so I started to think abut what they might want and how we could bring it to life. Any new film would have to show what the new tractors could do, and why they could do it better than any of products the company's competitors had ever produced. I was eventually shown a prototype which really was innovative and brilliant in its approach to lot of age old problems. I eventually produced a a treatment for a film which I thought might work. The story of our film would feature (and appear to be told by) the leader of a rival organisation's research and development team (who would be played by an actor). He had got wind of our client's plans for a new model and was determined to do everything he could to ensure it would never go on sale. He and a gang of carefully selected tough looking guys (also actors) would steal the prototype at dead of night and see what it as like. At the time *THE LADYKILLERS* film was doing good in British cinemas. Our audiences would witness the theft and follow the gang's attempts to find out what the new model was like. That would enable us to cover all the product's new sales points in a an interesting and entertaining way. In the end of course, it proved to be far better than anything they had ever envisaged. By developing that treatment I was confident we could get all David Brown's sales points across and and up with a valuable sales aid which would also be fun to watch. Since those happy days, when British made products were brand leaders all over the world, David Brown has been taken over by an American company. When they first moved in they knew relatively little about European requirements or farming methods. The new management was used to supplying huge farms in the USA. Today the factory we filmed in for so for many years has closed own and tractors are made in and imported from the USA. The heritage of one of Britain's most successful producers of agricultural equipment has been lost, and as a result, what would have been our next film was never made

As time passed the business we had started with a couple of pounds, and what we hoped might prove to be bankable ideas, gradually began to take off. When I left the BBC I had nothing. I was living in a rented room, did not own a car and was looking for a job though I knew what I eventually wanted to do, I realised it would not be easy to fulfil my ambitions, with no one to back me up and no track record to support my ever optimistic views. You may perhaps find yourself in a similar position. If you do, don't give up. It worked out alright for me and it will do for you, if you are aiming for the right goals and avoid making too many mistakes on route. After my first experience at the Rank Organisation and three years training with the BBC I, did at least know more about film and television production than I had done when I left school. After working in the industry when I had qualified, I had an even clearer picture of what I now wanted to do. The trouble was that I still had very little money and no connections in the areas I wanted to explore. I wrote lots of letters to individuals and organisations I felt might help me on my way. Most were ignored, but when I had scraped together enough to make my first films,which I described earlier it this book, doors began to open. At last I had something to show. If you are thinking of following a career like mine, the importance of learning basic skills, and then putting what you have learned into practice, by making a film to act as your shop window, cannot be overestimated. Today you can start a business at home with a laptop computer. You don't need plush premises or expensive gear. You do need ideas, energy and enthusiasm. When we started in 1964, we decided we needed an office in a central location. We knew that would be expensive so we rented office space by the hour! Adfone Business Services hired out rooms and had an address we thought we would rather like to have. They were in Regent Street - one of the smartest addresses in London's West End, two minutes walk from Piccadilly Circus. They provided us with our first office space. It was a room about six metres square with a wastepaper basket and a light. We arranged to hire it by the hour hour at a rate which we thought was excessive .It worked alright until one of the prestigious potential clients we had been chasing decided to pay us a visit.

Having seen our notepaper with a Regent Street address he arrived in a chauffeur driven car to learn that our office was on the fifth floor and the lift wasn't working. It wasn't a very auspicious start. Fortunately he was a very experienced man. He saw that we were young and he had done his homework He knew what we had and had not done and the questions he asked went straight to the point. He knew what we were all about. We were, as always, completely honest and told him what we did and did not have and what we hoped to do. He quietly listened to everything we said and then got up to leave.

A few days later we received a letter. It was from our first VIP guest. He thanked us for seeing him when had called. He then went on to explain that his company was about to sign a contract to supply a missile defence system to a Middle Eastern country. They were buying it second hand. It was at present in Germany but it would be dismantled and shipped to the country where their client was. For their records they wanted someone to film the whole operation, which they had code named *OPERATION MAGIC CARPET*. Would we be interested in quoting to do the job? I think you can guess our answer to that! We went on to win that contract and produce our first major overseas film in a country which then we had hardly heard about before - Saudi Arabia! A place we were to get to know much better in the years ahead.

While all this was going on we had kept in touch with our BBC friends and colleagues. The BBC had been very helpful to us. As I had worked for them and they had taught me most of the useful tricks I had learned, they felt they were in reasonably safe hands dealing with me. Our fledgling business became one of the first officially approved "outside" BBC production contractors - an accolade which was then not often bestowed. As a result we were given a number of jobs to do for various departments in the Corporation. I edited several films and my colleague - Alistair Cameron, who was and still is one of the best film cameramen in the business, shot some of their programmes on film.

At the time the BBC was without doubt the country's leading broadcaster. From its still pristine new Television Centre, to which a new wing had been added to accommodate BBC news, it produced a huge number of high quality programmes week after week. Some of the best talents in the business made shows there. David Croft and Jimmy Perry made *ARE YOU BEING SERVED?* while *THE GOOD LIFE* was being produced next door. In sport the BBC still showed many of the biggest national and international sporting events - a situation which was to continue until Sky Television produced a bigger chequebook. Even then, in my early days working on sport, we had been asked to think ahead and suggest sports which the Corporation might perhaps televise. I recall someone suggested darts and was regarded as a complete idiot. Another suggestion, that snooker might interest a few people and would be easy enough to do, was also greeted with contempt. Golf was however considered to be an excellent idea. There had been some limited golf coverage in the past but filming golf tournaments is expensive and requires a lot people and resources. Multi camera shoots are essential if the action is to be captured well and the techniques used up till then had been largely experimental. But things were changing fast. Ideas were put forward for a series of matches to be shot on film at championship courses. It was to be America versus the rest of the world and the world's top golfers would be invited to take part. The man put in charge of this new experiment was Phil Pilley - a very able BBC sports Producer and I had the pleasure of editing some of the programmes for him. The three main stars - Arnold Palmer, Gary Player and Jack Nicklaus were all a pleasure to work with. Laid back and knowing everything there is to know about golf, they took everything in their stride and performed just as well in howling gales and driving rain as they did when the sun was shining. Our film cameras, and the Mini Mokes we used to drive around the course, weren't so reliable and technology then was not nearly as advanced as it is today. The programmes took around four weeks each to make and they were a great success when they were shown. Some have now become television

television classics. In his own quietly efficient way Phil Pilley pioneered new way of doing things. He knew what to shoot, where to put his cameras and when to cut; which as every Producer knows is what making good television programmes is all about.

One of the heroes of that innovative series was the man who wrote and spoke the commentaries for most golfing events. Henry Longhurst was an immensely experienced Journalist who had lived long enough to become a golfing legend. When I first saw him, he was perched on a shooting stick in the middle of a course, waiting for his cue to commentate live on the match that was taking place. He looked as if he was asleep and had a hip flask in his hand, but when his cue came, he instantly and brilliantly summed up the whole day's play. Nothing was missed out and I was totally amazed. When he finished and knew he was off the air he looked at his watch, turned to me and said.

"Was that alright? They wanted a minute and I gave them 55 seconds. I think they should do." Now there are very few people who can do that!

HENRY LONGHURST

When I eventually decided to leave the BBC and set up in business with a few friends, the rot of John Birt's Producer Choice had not yet set in, though there were ominous clouds on the horizon. Staff were leaving at an ever increasing rate. Channel Four and Yorkshire Television claimed some of the BBC's greatest talents and others were going elsewhere at an ever increasing increasing rate. I felt I had got out at the right time. When later on it was announced that many of the programmes we had been able to produce so well in London would be moved to Salford I was delighted to be out. When that announcement was made, though staff were offered every inducement to move, a large number of well proven talents refused to budge. It also had a disastrous effect on people who were invited to appear in BBC programmes. While they were often happy to travel out to Television Centre at Shepherds Bush, traipsing up to one of the less attractive suburbs of Greater Manchester did not appeal to them at all. As a result, our recently established business grew much more quickly than it might otherwise have done. While we continued to do work for the BBC we also worked for several of the commercial; networks. When London Weekend Television first started, their temporary headquarters was an office block in Wembley. While their South Bank Studios were being built they rented cutting rooms from us. By that time we had bought the lease of a building in Covent Garden. It has been in the middle of what was then Covent Garden flower and vegetable market. When it moved to Nine Elms we bought the lease of a 5 storey building in Long Acre, just round the corner from the Royal Opera House. The ground floor and basement had been a fruit warehouse and the top floors offices. We converted the basement to a luxury preview theatre and the rest of the building to film cutting rooms. When we first moved into this prime central London spot I could drive in from my home in Ealing and park in the street outside to my office free of charge all day. When the market moved out that situation changed almost overnight but we remained there for many very happy years.

Our main business was, as I had always intended it to be, the production of commercially sponsored films. I had set that objective when we first started after seeing how other new film and television companies had fared in the preceding years. They and their suppliers had gone through tough times. Bank interest rates had reached 15% - not what you want when you are starting or running a business!

A significant number of new programme Producers had gone out of business in their first few months. They just found they were unable to compete. The big networks had studios and resident crews who knew they would get paid every week, even if they were not making programmes every day. Fledgling independent Producers cannot work like that. Today the situation has changed .The enormous overhead costs of running large studios has encouraged many broadcasters to buy in many of the programmes they transmit. They are made by specialist independent contractors (Indies like us and in due course perhaps you), or by freelance technicians working on short term contracts. If you are planning to start out as a Producer both these these changes will make it easier for you. There are more opportunities than there were when we started.Then everything was controlled by a relative handful or large companies. Bank interest rates are now at a sane levels. Which was not the case when we started with a couple of pounds and some ideas, and needed to borrow everything to start from scratch. That is why I decided to concentrate on making sponsored films. I have never felt happy taking unnecessary risks.

When that policy had started to pay off, I began to think about making other kinds of films. We had done well in our first foray into making commercially sponsored films and were now getting a regular flow of orders from well established companies. Repeat business was our bread and butter and that was fine with us. Though I was unaware of it at the time, we had yet to discover the market that was transform my life and business. In the meantime we had to decide what we should do at the point we had reached. We had said goodbye to our first rented office space and acquired and equipped our own five storey building in the heart of London's West End. We had a good list of regular clients, most of whom had become friends. We had deliberately remained a small team, who enjoyed what we were doing. I had recruited a wonderful Secretary - Margaret Sylvester - who somehow managed to to read my writing and type our scripts for years before computers arrived on the scene. When she left us to get married we felt we had lost a key member of the team but I am pleased to say that today, over 30 years later, we are still in touch and she is still a delight to know. In our first few years we had to learn the difference between need and want. When we started we *wanted* to have the biggest office desks, plush premises and the latest equipment. We soon learned that what we actually *needed* was not the things we read about in glossy magazines. As you too will discover, in our business you can hire most professional film making equipment on a long or short term basis. You don't need to go out and spend loads of cash. The latest model can usually wait until it is cheaper. What you do need is endless enthusiasm, hard work and ideas. When we reached the happy stage where our Bank Manager smiled when he saw us in stead of asking if we had an account, we knew we had turned the first of many corners and could consider starting to expand. The big question was *how*. So many businesses have gone bankrupt as a direct result of expanding too fast, and we did not want to run that risk. I was keen to make television programmes again, but not at the expense of giving up what we had shown could be a lucrative business.- sponsored films. Though sometimes looked at with contempt, by those who think films start and finish with James Bond, they can be a key to success. They can also give you a good standard of living without all the worries often associated with making feature films. You will not see your name in lights in Leicester Square but you are likely to have a longer and more lucrative career than many who fall off the tracks before their names appear in lights. With those thoughts in mind, I started to try and think of television programme ideas which I thought we could do well with the limited finance and resources we had available.

That ruled out contributing to any network's peak time viewing on a regular basis. Big drama series or shows with large casts or expensive sets were clearly not for us. It was difficult to think of anything we could do and hope to sell. Then, even more so than today, television networks preferred to buy complete series. A package of six or twelve of programmes, each running for thirty or sixty minutes was much easier to sell than a one off show. Documentaries were particularly hard to interest anyone in, though regional showings were sometimes easier to achieve. I wanted to do something I knew we could do well and would enjoy doing. I also knew it would have to be made without breaking the bank. It would be nice if we could also have a chance of getting our money back!

My interest in sponsored films has been begun when in my first job at The Rank Organisation I had noticed how successful their sponsored films were. They, and the industrial training programmes they distributed alongside their main catalogue of feature films, were always in demand. That point had remained in the back of my mind for several years but it as not to have its full impact for several more years yet. Eventually the penny did drop and I was able to cash in on the developments I had first witnessed then. My years with the BBC had taught me how to make television programmes but they had not left me with bundles full of cash. So I had to try to find a television package we could make with limited resources and hope to sell. It took two years to put together a project which I thought might work.

As large budgets and extravagant shows were clearly going to be out, my mind turned to what had been one of the BBC's most successful and long running shows. It was what is generally described as a chat show. A programme built around a well known personality or star being interviewed, usually by someone who was himself a star or at least a well known household name. The BBC's star performer in that field was a Yorkshire man - Michael Parkinson, who had left school with two O levels and a passion for cricket.

For over thirty years he interviewed the good, bad and completely hopeless, brilliantly, live on television, and managed to remain a very nice man! Having watched his shows being produced I knew how much effort had been involved. Months of research and a large production team with many different talents, and the use of some of the BBC's best studios and back up resources. No expense was spared and the shows were always a pleasure to watch. When I was looking round for something I felt we could do, the chat show format appealed to me because I thought it could be done in a different way and at much lower cost using less resources. I envisaged a programme where the interviewer would never appear. He (or she) might be heard but would never be seen. The camera(s) would concentrate on the subject of the film. The programme would include stills and as much additional material as we could find if it was relevant to what was being said. It would not include clips from feature films or other productions which could involve royalty payments and detract from the simple format I wanted to explore.

I planned to shoot all the shots I thought we needed then retire to our cutting rooms, put it all together and see if I could make it work. As we did not have enough money to pay anyone well known to ask the questions it would have to be me off camera doing that job. I would cut them out when editing and then write a linking, commentary to set the scene, link shots together and provide any information audiences might want to know and not find in the subject's own comments. I knew that would be breaking new ground and would probably encounter opposition at every point but it was way I wanted to try and see if it would work. I knew our biggest problem in getting my ideas that off the ground would be in persuading anyone worth knowing to take part.

When I worked out a framework for the show, I also made a tentative list of some of the people I wanted to appear. They were all big names. The sort of people who had appeared or refused to appear on Parkinson's show and were sought after by Reporters all over the world. Unlike the BBC, I could not pick up a phone, call on the services of a huge production team and make my first approach from a position of authority. We were nobodies. I was aware of that, but I had made my list and was young enough to have confidence in an idea I thought could work. As we had nothing to lose I decided to go ahead and see what reactions I got. My list included many famous names, none of whom I knew at that time. Top of the list was a major film star who had recently won an Oscar. He had also written an autobiographical book which had been at the top of the best seller lists in the UK and USA for nearly two years, setting a new record. His last major film - Michael Todd's production of *AROUND THE WORLD IN 80 DAYS* - had been the hottest ticket in town. For several days I tried to work out how I could approach him. From my BBC experience I knew that if they made that call they would be told to contact his Agent. In a few months time, negotiations involving lots of different people, would result in him either agreeing or refusing to take part. His name was David Niven and I k n e w that in the course of his work he travelled a lot and had homes in Switzerland and in France, where he had bought a beautiful house at Cap Ferrat. It had once belonged to Charlie Chaplin, who was not noted for his generosity when it came to household repairs. When Niven moved in he had to spend a lot of money putting things right. He turned it into one of the gems of the French Riviera. I had been given a telephone number and, after several sleepless nights, decided to call it. After ringing for what seemed like for ever, my call was answered by a man who only spoke French. I had done reasonably well in languages at school and knew that I now had to find out if it had been worth the effort. Would the man I was speaking to understand what I wanted to say? Fortunately he did and I knew enough to understand "Attendez", and that was as far as our conversation went. I was left handing on…. and on.

I wondered if I ought to hang up but, after taking so long to get the number and make the call I decided to wait. Eventually another voice emerged. This one spoke English and that gave me confidence. As briefly as I could I gave him my name and explained the purpose of my call. I just said I would like to talk to Mr Niven and had a television programme I would like him to do. Would it be possible to arrange to a meet so we could discuss the project? There was a long pause. Just when I was beginning to think we had reached the end of my call, the voice at the other end started asking questions. He wanted to know who I was and what company I worked for. I explained that I had recently started a small independent company to make films for television. He then asked what I had made before. I told him about my BBC years and he listened but made no comment. Then there was a pause. I thought that he had gone but, as I was about to hang up in despair, he spoke again. "I am away quite a lot but if you want to come over I will listen to what you have got to say. Send me a telex and let me know when you want to come, and we can take it from there." It was only then that I realised I had been speaking to the man himself - The one and only David Niven.

A few days later I was called by an aide who explained that Mr Niven had told him to call and make an appointment for us to meet. He suggested the arrivals section of Nice airport might be the most convenient location for all concerned. On the date we agreed I caught an Air France Caravelle from London Heathrow to Nice. I arrived at mid day and walked across the tarmac to the terminal building. I was the last off the plane and when I reached the arrivals section most of the other passengers had already left. They knew the way. I did not, so I followed the signs and moved towards the end of the building. It looked deserted and I was beginning to think that I had been living in a dream and would soon wake up and find I was still at Heathrow. I was about to go to the ticket desk and book a flight back to London when a man in dark glasses emerged from the the shadows.

He walked towards me at a brisk pace, stopped and spoke. "Is your name Burder?" he asked. I confirmed that it was. He removed his glasses and I came face to face for the first time with David Niven.

We got on well from that first meeting. Over a delightful lunch in a small seaside restaurant near the airport (which he insisted on paying for) we chatted about what I had come to discuss. I thanked him for being kind enough to see me and we talked and laughed together. A big star he undoubtedly was but David Niven was above all a delightfully normal and very pleasant man. He told me he understood what I wanted to do and remembered the problems he had experienced when he had started his career. He said he had failed almost everything at school and only started to enjoy life when he got nought out of a hundred in his naval entrance exams and was sent in stead to a new English public school - Stowe. Its founding Headmaster - R.F.Roxburgh, who was to become one of the most respected names in education, had encouraged Niven to stand up for himself and coached him through the entrance exams for the Royal Military Academy at Sandhurst. He never forgot the help he had been given and he told me that, later in life, when he was a Hollywood star, he still used to consult Roxbugh on situations where he felt he needed some advice..

We eventually shot our film in the garden of his house overlooking the sea at Cap Ferrat. Away from the restraints of a studio and large crews, he was able to relax and sound as if he was just talking to friends, which is what I had hoped would happen when I devised my overall programme format. We filmed for two days stopping only to eat and refresh ourselves with excellent local wine. We used two cameras shooting continuously alongside each other. They were loaded with 16mm Eastmancolour film. Sound was recorded on a bank of Nagra broadcast quality tape recorders, linked to the camera which were set up alongside.

David and I sat facing each other with his garden in the background, me out of frame and the shot concentrating on him. We got on well, as we had when we first met, and had two very pleasant days. We had a six man camera and sound crew, who were used to working with each other. They knew what they were doing, which saved time and avoided any technical problems in the course of the shoot. I had spent three weeks preparing a list of the topics I wanted David to talk about. I decided not to include any feature film clips. Unlike other chat shows,I wanted to avoid showing our audiences short bits of films they had probably seen many times before. My aim was to explore what those films had been like from David's point of view. What had he needed to do when they were being made? What were the people he was working with like from his point of view? If we could explore those points in the right way in some depth I felt we would end up with an interesting programme After the first morning filming it was clear that we stood a good chance of doing that.

David, who had completely relaxed in surroundings he knew so well, recalled things and events he had did not often mention. He spoke of his experiences as an Officer Cadet at Sandhurst, and the mistakes he had made there in that very junior rank. When we finished our filming in France, I was able to persuade the then Commanding Officer of Sandhurst to reconstruct some of the parades David had recalled, using his latest intake of new cadets. That footage was included in our final film. It brought David's words to life and was much better than watching someone in a studio, under lots of lights, surrounded by technicians.

From Sandhurst David has gone into the army and started a career as a regular soldier. It was not as straightforward as that may sound. In our film and he recalled some of the gaffes he had made in his early days. As the modest man he was, he conveniently forgot to mention that he had gone on to serve with distinction in the second world war. I was able to fill in those gaps later with material I had already obtained elsewhere. He went to America for the first time in the 1930s. It was prohibition time and booze was off limits almost everywhere in town. David wanted to become an actor but did not know anyone who could help him to get started. He got a job "selling bootleg booze at some pretty sleazy joints." A chance meeting with society Hostess Elsa Maxwell lead to his first introduction to the world of films. A few weeks later he was employed as an "Extra". His union card described him as "Anglo Saxon type 2008." In that capacity he first appeared on screen. After weeks of waiting for something to come up, he was eventually allowed to speak one line. He said "Hello my Dear," to an actress who was getting off a train." He remembered that he was "such a smash at that" that a few weeks later he was given another line, and had to say "Goodbye my Dear" to another actress who was boarding another train!" His big break came when he was asked to appear in the MGM film of *WUTHERING HEIGHTS*. It starred Laurence Olivier and Merle Oberon - two of the biggest stars at that time. Niven was cast as Edgar - a notoriously difficult part with very few lines. The film was directed by William Wyler - one of the biggest names in the business, who later went on to direct *MRS MINIVER* and a host of other Oscar winning films. He was know to be a tough man for actors to work with and he and David fell out from day one.

In our film he recalled how his confidence had been shattered when Wyler directed him in a bedside scene which has since become a movie classic. With Merle Oberon playing a character dying in bed and Laurence Olivier standing alongside, Niven had to kneel at the foot of the bed, lean, forward and cry. It was his first real test as an actor and, with all the cast and crew watching, he found he was unable to cry on demand. Wyler was furious. He hated delays and and called in a special effects man who sprayed menthol into Niven's face and eyes. " Now lean over the bed, screw up your eyes and cry!" Wyler commanded, as everybody watched. In our film David recalled what happened then.

"In stead of tears, green slime shot out of my nose, all over the corpse lying in the bed. Merle shot up and ran off the set. It was all very traumatic."

By lunch time it was clear that we were getting something rather good and that situation continued for the rest of our shoot. As it neared its end, David recalled how he had won his one and only Oscar for his performance in the film version of Terence Rattigan's play *SEPARATE TABLES*.

We ended our filmed conversation with his recollections of working with one of the cinema's movie moguls - Michael Todd, who produced many successful shows and films including *AROUND THE WORLD IN 80 DAYS*. At the time Todd was married to Elizabeth Taylor. They were the hottest properties in show business gossip. David recalled how he had enjoyed playing his role as Phileas Fogg so much that he would have done it for nothing. In that part he had worked with another major star and had helped him to get his role. In our film he explained how that had come about. His account was later lost when the original full length version of our film was re cut to make an updated version. In the middle of that edit the laboratory which had processed our original film was sold for redevelopment. One can of film was lost at that time. It was the one which contained Niven's sad but true story about his friend and co star. So, perhaps I can repeat what he said as I think his words are well worth recalling.

One of the other key characters in *AROUND THE WORLD IN 80 DAYS* is a rogue detective - Mr Fix, who was played in the film by Robert Newton. When the production of the film as first announced, Newton had not been seen on screen for several years. There was of course a reason for that and it was a reason of which Producer Michael Todd was well aware. When Niven suggested Newton should play Mr Fix, Todd was dead against the idea. He summed up his objections in a few words. "Your pal Newton is a lush. He is no good." And that as far as he was concerned, was the end of that.

For months David kept up the pressure and eventually Todd gave in and Newton got the job provided he agreed "to sign the pledge."

As our filming session in his garden ended, David recalled what happened next.

"The film took two years to complete and Bobby was marvellous in it. He never touched a drop and gave the performance of his life. It was all over and then we were called back to do a retake. I arrived at the studio and I could hear Bobby, some distance away. He was in full flight, with the *Once more into the breach* speech. Full volume! Unable to stand up.! It was so sad. He as a great actor and a lovely man. He died a few just a few months Later."

When our film was finished it was very well received. Canadian Television (CBC) were the first to show it. The last was, of course, the UK! It has recently been updated and digitally restored, so future generation will be able to appreciate the talents of a remarkable man.

ROBERT NEWTON and DAVID NIVEN

FROM THE ARCHIVES
DAVID NIVEN
LOOKING BACK
FILM RECENTLY RESTORED

Back at home the pressure was increasing for us to make make more sponsored films. That was fine because it meant they would be self financing but deciding which subjects to a do and which to turn down was sometimes a difficult task. High budget productions were always of interest for obvious reasons but many other subjects had merits of their own. In the following months we produced films on a wide range of subjects. Two stand out I my mind as they were both rather special. One resulted from an enquiry made by a lady who had been almost paralysed with pain since she was born. The other became part of history and brought us in close contact with Britain's Prime Minister on what was probably the most difficult of her life.

As I mentioned earlier, films can do a lot of different jobs. Our Niven film, made for television, was designed to entertain. Our next production had a completely different aim. It set out to raise funds to help people whose interests are too often ignored by almost everyone. As a film maker, one of the privileges you can enjoy is the ability to help people who are less well off than yourself. I have always been interested in trying to support worthwhile causes and have tried to use the few skills I have to help them, just as I do when I am asked to make films by some of or most successful businesses in the land.

When I first met the lady I mentioned just now, she was smiling from ear to ear. Alice was always smiling, which was surprising because the slightest move or change of expression could be agony to her. She was in her eighties when we first met. She had been born with rheumatoid arthritis and had found it difficult to move from day one. People generally associate arthritis with old age but it also affects children and there is no known cure. Alice lived with her family until they died. Then she was all on her own. She lived in accommodation which the council provided, but that was as far as their interest went. Day after day, for 24 hours she stayed in the same place with the same outlook of other peoples' dustbins and a brick wall. As I started to get to know her

I noticed that, when things went wrong she always made the best of it and got on with what had to be done. Her life was made bearable by a charity which, once a week came to take her out in a specially equipped vehicle. It was basically a truck with an electric hoist at the back and spaced out seats inside. It did not look much but to Alice it was the key to freedom and a yellow brick road which lead directly to the Wizard of Oz. The wizard in this case was a local organisation which a ran a day centre where people like Alice could come, enjoy a meal, talk to others and be entertained. Her weekly trips had transformed her life and she asked me to go and see what she got up to on her days out. I accepted her invitation and a saw the wonderful work that was being done. I eventually made a film about what I had seen. Its aim was to raise funds so more could be done. I am glad to say it achieved its objective and was a success. As a film maker you too can benefit and help other people, by making films to promote good causes. There is a lot of pleasure in helping people who cannot afford much, to benefit from opportunities you can help provide.

The second film we made at that point brought us in touch with a very different lady. We had been asked by a client of ours to make a film to mark a milestone in the history of a company he had set up 21 year before. They were about to expand and planned to open a vast new office and warehouse complex at their north London headquarters. There would be a big party and the new premises would be officially opened by the local MP, who had been involved with the company since it had started. On the day before the event was due to take place we called to Check that it would take place as planned. We were assured it would but were advised that the Guest of Honour, who was to perform the opening ceremony, might be changed as the VIP they expected might "be otherwise engaged." We thought no more about it. Having filmed lots of opening ceremonies and VIPs of one kind or another, that sort of thing was par for the course. The following day we arrived at our client's new premises to find what looked like half the world's press queuing up outside trying to get in.

We fought our way through police and security and were eventually allowed to drive our camera car though double locked gates. Once inside we were welcomed by the owner of the business whose big day it was. Michael Gerson was, and still is one of the most successful businessmen of his day. He started an international removals company with virtually nothing and built it into one of the most successful companies around. His local MP, who had been a loyal supporter from his first days, had agreed to open the new warehouse in half an hour's time. Behind locked doors Mr Gerson then told us why half the world's press was clamouring outside. The event was private and entry by invitation only. Their Guest of Honour had been slightly delayed but had just confirmed that any delay would not be long and events should proceed as planned. We were then told that the reason there had been a delay was because the Guest of Honour was Margaret Thatcher - Britain's Prime Minster, who had chaired a cabinet meeting earlier that morning as a task force of ships had sailed from Southampton to the Falklands Islands. To everyone's surprise, the events of that day proceeded as planned. Denis Thatcher arrived, in his pale blue Ford, and parked it in a secure place. (He had apparently been advised to sell the Rolls Royce he had loved and owned for years when his wife became Prime Minister.) At 11.30 am the Guest of Honour duly arrived, looking completely calm and in control on what must surely have been the hardest day of her life. For two hours we filmed everything that happened. Mrs Thatcher made a speech, toured the new building and met customers and and staff. She took a real interest in everything she saw and never appeared to be in a rush. After a excellent lunch in the new warehouse building, which had been suitably equipped, a Royal Marines band brought proceedings to a close. The Guest of Honour left and we went back edit our film. Now thirty years later, it has just been digitally restored. It is the only record of an historic event and it has now been preserved for for future generations.

STAR
May 20,1982: The day the talking stopped
IN WE GO
Admiral Sandy gets the order: Hit them early and har

FROM THE ARCHIVES
Programme 5
MARGARET THATCHER
STANDARD
21 killed as British helicopter ditches in sea... nine rescued
TROOPS GO INTO ACTION
20TH CENTURY BRITAIN PRESERVED FOR FUTURE GENERATIONS

One of the most interesting films I was asked to produce in my early years as an independent film Producer continues to be in demand, even though its visual images are obviously well out of date. When it was made, it featured what were then some of the latest cars. Now they are old hat, but the message of the film is as strong now as it ever was and today it has become something of a cult. It has recently been digitally restored and now, if it is introduced by a suitably qualified person who is familiar with the subject the film is about, it it can be as effective now as when it was first produced.

As the story of how it came to be made contains lessons for would-be film Producers (*How to deal with difficult Sponsors*) and for relatively inexperienced film Producers (*How to win the day, get business and satisfy everyone without losing your cool*) I will tell you how it came about.

DRINK AND DRIVE? was first released in 1967 - the year in which a blood alcohol level limit for drivers first became enforceable by law. The film was sponsored by a consortium of insurance companies. Their spokesman was a strict teetotaller who believed anything to do with alcohol was the work of the devil. I was then one of the youngest television Producers around. Like many people at that time, I had never thought about alcohol and driving and used to enjoy the odd pint when I finished work. There were then no laws against what had always been an acceptable way of of life. Our sponsor's spokesman had very definite views on everything in life and knew exactly what our film should do." You must put the fear of God into anyone who drinks and drives", he told me over a glass of orange juice when we first met."The only way to get our message across is to scare them to death." I asked if he had anything particular I mind. Without pausing for breath he then outlined a complete scenario which he had worked out." You have got to start with a uniformed Policeman, so they know what he is saying is enforceable by law. He must give some statistics. Casualty figures for accidents which occur when people drink too much." And so he went on... and on, until, I had a very clear idea of what he had in mind. I thought about it overnight and the next day said I would not make the film. They would have to find someone else. I heard no more for a couple of weeks and then I got a call, asking if we could meet again. I thought it would be interesting to know who had got the job, and felt I could face another orange juice, so a meeting was arranged. This time I found I was dealing with a rather different man. He was prepared to listen to what I had to say.

" I know you don't like my ideas" he said and then added ," So what would you do?" And he left it at that.

Before you read on, if you are thinking of becoming a film Producer you may care to pause for a few moments and think how you would have dealt with his point. *What would **you** have said and done at that point to achieve what he clearly wanted to do. I will then tell you what I did in the paragraphs which follow.*

I told him that I thought starting with what we call a "talking head" (his uniformed Policeman talking to camera) was probably the best way of sending his audience to sleep. Talking down to anyone rarely makes friends and in a film, which must clearly appeal to young people if it is to succeed, I felt there were better ways to begin. As a relatively young man I thought then, and have not changed my views, that if people are to be persuaded to do or believe something they need to be given enough evidence to know what it is all about. Then they can make their own decisions. How that evidence is presented is crucial . When you are making a film there are usually a number of ways you can get a message across. My teetotal friend had one. After a lot of research I was able to come up with another.

I assumed audiences would be as ignorant as I was. They needed to know *why*, and how the new law would affect them and their lives. They did not want an authoritative figure telling them it was wrong. They needed to know why and, to explain that, I devised a treatment which I thought might work.

With the help of police forces across the country, I was given access to hundreds of reports on road accidents in which alcohol was thought to have been a crucial factor. I analysed those reports, noting the type of vehicles involved, what had occurred and who had been driving at the time. I then knew who our film must address. I then managed to locate a university Professor who had spent several years carrying out research into the effects of alcohol on the human body. He was an acknowledged expert on what to any outsider is a fairly complex subject. I now had a clear idea of the kind of audiences we needed to address

The next question to be resolved was how to do it. I outlined my suggestions over another glass of orange juice.

"I don't think it's an use telling people it is wrong. We have got to show why." I then went on to suggest that we should stage a practical demonstration of what can happen if excessive amounts of alcohol are consumed by people who then drive.

"If we could could take over a runway on a disused airfield" (I had one in mind) "and arrange an obstacle course for drivers, which includes some of the hazards they are likely to find driving to work or on a school run, I think we could do something people will believe. My proposal is that we should put several drivers in the same kind of cars and ask them to drive round the course we have devised three times. On the first occasion they will be completely sober. They will then be given carefully measured doses of alcohol before they drive round again. After a suitable interval they will be given more alcohol and then drive round again. We will film all the drives with cameras outside and inside each car to record what happens. As they negotiate the course the drivers will hear a tape which will ask them some basic questions on everyday life. That will simulate the effects of talking to any passengers who might be travelling with them. And then we will see what a happens." My unusually silent companion was clearly hooked. It took us a while to get ready to film. We found a deserted airfield in in Leicestershire. I enlisted the help of the police and the Automobile Association. The Ford Motor Company kindly agreed to lend us some cars. I had one of the best camera and sound teams around and we set out to capture everything on film.

We shot for two days in a bitterly cold wind and driving rain, which made everything difficult to film. In between drives, our test drivers, who had been recruited from local universities and colleges, were given carefully measured mixtures of vodka and orange juice under medical supervision. They were not told if they they were or were not consuming alcohol. I directed operations by radio from a windswept puddle in the middle of it all. The whole exercise was completely genuine. Nothing was fixed and no one knew what the results would reveal.

Some drivers performed better after their first drink but as time passed and the level of alcohol they had consumed increased, they began to fall apart, as our film showed. It was very revealing. When he finished shooting, I thought that some audiences might still not be totally convinced. With that in mind I showed some of our footage to the police forces who had helped us to set up our tests and asked what they thought. They all said it confirmed everything they knew and came across in their everyday work. I then asked if they could dig through their records and find real life incidents where the blood alcohol levels of those involved had been the same as those of the drivers featured in our tests. When they came back with the facts, with their permission I contacted the people who had been involved in in those incidents and asked they would allow us to reconstruct what had actually happened. Meeting the relatives of those who had died brought the subject of our film home to me in ways I shall never be able to forget. I have not touched any alcoholic drink when know I am going to have to drive in the next 24 hours, from that day to this.

In the weeks which followed our airfield shoot, we reconstructed the incidents we had been given permission to stage. It was a heartbreaking task. We had to be very accurate in everything we showed. One of the incidents we staged involved a young man who had a row with his girlfriend and went out to get drunk. On his way back from a pub he misjudged a bend on a road he knew well. His car careered off the road and ended in a river. His body was found the following day. We had to reconstruct that accident.

To do that we had to find the same make of car, which we could write off. We then had to remove the engine and drain out every trace of oil so it would not pollute the river when it was lowered into it by crane. The crane was then removed and the car allowed to sink, as if it had just crashed. We then we had to find another identical car which could still be driven so we could shoot the earlier driving scenes.

In the finished film we simply stated the facts. The blood alcohol level of the driver who died that night was the same as the last driver we had seen in our tests. The one who thought he was alright to drink and drive.

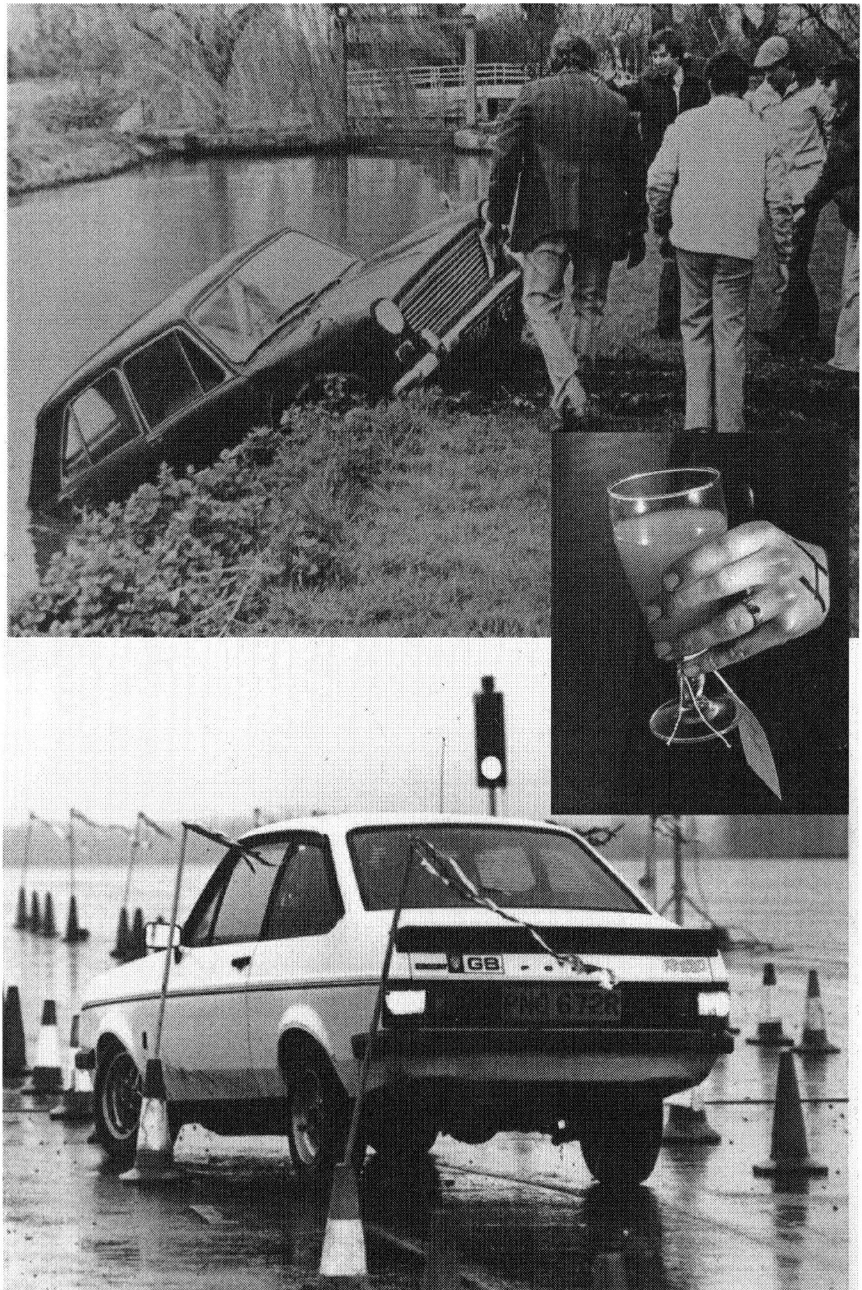
GB

As you will discover if you decide to become a film Producer, you are only as good as your last film. That is what I was told when I started my own business. I eventually found out that it wasn't entirely true. As you make more and more films, there is generally at east one which should be good enough to encourage others to come to you. If there is not, you are probably in the wrong job for you. The point the person who made that remark to me was trying to make was that, when you have a success, people will want to climb aboard and work with you. If you make disaster after disaster you could end up on your own. *DRINK AND DRIVE?* was my first venture into what was to become a major part of our ever growing business. I was used to making television programmes to interest and entertain. That film, which we had shot in two days in a freezing wind and driving rain, was designed to do a completely different job. It was meant to help save lives.

As I mentioned in the earlier chapter in this book, one of the attractions of a media career is that you are unlikely to be doing the same thing day after day. In some cases you may do something once and never again. That is what makes life interesting. There is always something new to learn. *DRINK AND DRIVE* had safety as its theme. Road safety in that case, but it was to involve me in safety issues in many other ways. When we set up in business as independent Producers of films for television and industry, we wondered what sort of films we ought to produce. We considered all the obvious kinds, but what was to become one our biggest money spinners, and change my life for ever, we did not think about at all. At that time, safety was beginning to be more than just a word we all heard about at school. Industries were starting to get involved and governments had began to realise that accidents at home and at work were costing taxpayers millions of pounds a year. In other countries the same point was also being made. When the European Union was formed, the safety business really started to take off. Before that, in the 1950s and 60s, Safety Officers had often tended to be people who were given their jobs because they did not fit in anywhere else. They were retired Officers from the services, who were used to managing people but often had no first hand experience of what their employers actually did. They were regarded as a safe pair of hands and had often reached an age where they were not considered to be worth training for other posts. When the Health and Safety At Work Act became law, that situation changed almost overnight. Millions of pounds were poured into into safety related businesses, and that was when when I thought we should climb aboard.

The safety and training films market at that time was dominated by two big companies. Millbank Films - a subsidiary of one of the UK's biggest companies - ICI (Imperial Chemical Industries) made excellent safety films. Another company, headed by a man who had also worked for the BBC but in in a different capacity to me, made training films on a number of other subjects Their production were mostly concerned with sales training and management. They too were very good indeed. The man who starred in many of their films, and was also involved in running the business was actor John Cleese.

Both the organisations I have just mentioned had far more resources than us. They also had very plush premises and seemingly unlimited funds. I loved what they were doing but still felt we might be able to do something if we went about it in the right way.

At this point I am again going to suggest that ,if you are a budding film Producer, you may care to put this book aside for a few moments and consider what *you* would have done at that point. Would you have abandoned any idea of making safety or training films ? Would you have dismissed safety as just a passing fad? Or would you have made films for the UK and/or overseas? If you chose the last course, what would your films have been about and what do you think would have made them work? In the paragraphs which follow I will explain what we did, so you can decide if we were right or wrong.

I had noted that our two main competitors both employed well know actors to appear in their films. They also had some of the best scriptwriters who had written their television shows. They created characters audiences would be able to identify with. Their films were expertly made and did an excellent job. They were also costly to produce because a lot of expensive talents were involved. And there was another point which I thought we might be able to improve on. Most of the scenes in our competitors' films featured characters who appeared on screen and spoke English. The situations shown were also very British throughout. That meant they could not be used overseas without costly dubbing. Their Producers, of course, felt that, as they were UK companies, that did not matter. Their job was to sell in the UK. I did not have the backing of ICI or wealthy investors. I needed to reach as big a market as I could. I also wanted to make films which could be updated easily at reasonable cost - a consideration which has paid substantial dividends over many years. And there was another key decision which had to be made. If you decide you want to be a film Producer it is one you too may face. Did we want to make commercially sponsored training films, with money up front or could we recover our production costs by selling what we had produced. Sometimes it is possible to combine both those objectives, and that is what we did with some of our training films. As that meant we did not have to find massive sums up front you may care to know what we did and how it worked out.

The first secret of success is to pick the right subject to film. Tadpole breeding in rural areas is not a good subject, in case that is one which had crossed your mind! As always when you are running a business, your potential market is the point to consider first. Unless you are happy to put your hand in your pocket ,and go on pouring out cash for ever more, you need to do your sums before you start. In practical terms, for any film Producer, that means you have got to pick a subject and find a sponsor who will put of all or part of the production cost, or be confident that enough people will be interested in whatever you decide to make, to enable you you to recover your costs (with a worthwhile profit.) Here are a couple of examples of how that can be done.

When I was looking for a subject for our first independent safety training film, I wanted to find something which concerned, (or should concern) as many people as possible. At that time, my local newspaper was carrying a report on a big factory fire. It had broken out in the middle of the afternoon. Workers had been trapped as their offices filled with smoke and extensive damage had been caused. That report gave me my starting point. Fires can involve anyone, anywhere, at any time, so we all need to be prepared. That would be the basic message of our film. I decided to make a general fire safety training film which could be used on all kinds of industrial and commercial premises. Factories, offices, shops and other business premises would all be able to benefit from its message which their staff would be able to learn from and hopefully enjoy. With that in mind I did some research. My own knowledge of fires at that time was largely based on burning the toast. I knew nothing about what fires cost or how they started. As always, I decided to tap the minds of experts who knew what they were talking about. I chose six very senior Fire Officers and persuaded them to act as our Technical Advisors. The resulting film, first released under the title of *THE ABC OF FIRE*, has been updated many times over the years. It has recently been digitally restored and released again as *ALL ABOUT FIRE,* but it is basically the same film, simply because it worked so well. It is periodically updated because there have been changes in legislation and in the ways we work and live. Smoking is now banned on most commercial premises. It was one of the major causes of fires at work. Fire extinguishers all used to be colour coded. They were blue, black or red, depending on their content. Now all extinguishers are red. EEC regulations decided that, but people still need to know what they contain and what they will and will not do. Regular updates took care of that.

181

Our first training film was a success because it covered the right points in ways which were interesting to watch. People found it helped them, and they still do today. Updated versions in various languages are still in demand and the film has recovered its initial production costs many times. It has also brought us a lot of new business from people who liked what we had done. Two of the biggest companies making fire extinguishers asked us to make films about their products. We showed how they were made and produced training films for them, which they were able to sell and use to run their own training programmes. We also made a number specialist films for different kinds of audiences. That is another area you may care to explore. We made a separate film about fires in hotels. It dealt with problems particular to them. The Home Office liked what we had done and gave us another job. Prisons contain many flammable materials and some desperate people. Fires in prisons are not uncommon. The Home Office asked us to make a film to show Prison Officers what they should do if a fire broke out on their premises. We did that well enough for one of the Britain' biggest railway companies to approach us. They were having problems with drunken passengers setting fire to carriages, in half empty trains, late at night. Two carriages had recently been badly damaged. So far no one had been seriously injured, but the company's staff needed to know what they should do to prevent a disaster if they were in charge. Our film took them through the steps they should take one by one. Over the years we have handled many different assignments to meet the specific needs of clients all over the world. As a result, we have one of the most comprehensive libraries of fire and safety shots and sounds which we are always striving to keep up to date.

When we had captured a large part of the safety training market, we decided to look at other kinds of training films. Here again we found opportunities you too could explore if you decide you want to become a film Producer. Perhaps you are a Trainer who has a specialist knowledge of a particular job or subject. If you make or commission a film, you could put your knowledge and experience across to a much wider audience.

You might be surprised by what you could achieve. Good training films can make a lot of money. If they are badly made or have the wrong aims, they can also lose everything invested in them.

One of the most successful training films we produced, dealt with a subject which sounds so mundane and dull many film Producers would not give it a thought. That subject is manual handling. Now I would be the first to agree that, if your you are looking for an Oscar or want your name in lights outside the Odeon Leicester Square, that may not be the right subject to film. If on the other hand , you are looking for a subject for a film which can make money for you for over thirty years, and appeal to audiences in 27 countries, you could be missing out. I can tell you from experience that, if you ignore dull subjects you do so at your peril. The dullest subjects can be made interesting to watch and they can sometimes bring in rich rewards.

THE COMMON SENSE GUIDE TO
MANUAL HANDLING

Our *COMMON SENSE GUIDE TO MANUAL HANDLING* came into being when I was met a man who had recently lost his job. He had been lifting a box from a trolley to a rack. The box was heavier than he thought it would be and, when it was half way between the trolley and the rack he had felt a sudden pain in his back and it had been with him ever since. As he could not work he was not being paid and he was naturally very upset.

I soon discovered that he was not alone. Incidents like that occur somewhere almost every day. The damage is done in seconds but it does not end there. Back injures can can take a long time to heal. As a result they can end up costing employers and employees a lot of money and give them problems which could often have been avoided by taking a few simple steps. That, I thought, should be the main message of our film. We did not need big name actors or elaborate scenes and sets. We just had to show what should and should not be done in a clear and interesting way. And that is what we did.

When you are dealing with safety, as with many other subject in which experts and so called experts are often involved, you will often find someone who thinks he or she knows better than everyone else. "Experts" don't always agree on every point. As we wanted to do everything we could to ensure we got the messages across, we involved six of Europe's most experienced Safety Officers when we were writing the script. When the film was shot they supervised every set up and checked every point. When shooting was completed we showed the rushes to some more Safety Officers and asked what they thought. Only when we had unanimous approval on every point and it has been approved by a team of lawyers was the film released.

Since it was first released it has been used by thousands of organisations around the world. The latest version we have released is in Mandarin Chinese. Like many of our other production, we try to keep it reasonably up to date. It has recently been digitally enhanced but the content remains much as it originally was. We did once make a couple of major changes but so many people told us it was better as it was we went back to the original. Where handling techniques have changed as a result of new regulations, we have generally tried to take note of that but otherwise we have been guided by the people who have used our film day after day, sometimes for years, without complaints. We called our film *THE COMMON SENSE GUIDE TO MANUAL* HANDLING because that is what it is!. We did not set out to be clever. We just wanted to help ordinary people by alerting them to the sort of things which can cause injuries, and show how those injuries can be avoided. By not twisting and turning when you are carrying a load. By not carrying too much and by always lifting and lowering whatever you are carrying in a safe way. Nothing extravagant. Nothing grand. Perhaps that is why it has worked so well!

While we were busily involved in meeting an ever growing number of requests to make commercially sponsored films, our television programme on David Niven was being very well received. People really seemed to like it. I was keen to make more programmes using the format I had devised, which we had proved worked very well. I was also aware that many businesses had bankrupted themselves by expanding too fast. I did not want to risk everything we had managed to achieve so far by trying to finance a project which I knew might bring us down. Bank interest rates were then at 15%!

We did make three more television programmes without breaking the bank. The three we made did well and they have recently been digitally restored, so future generations will be able to appreciate the talents of the artistes who were involved.

They included Vincent Price was then the undisputed king of horror movies. We also made a great show with Tommy Steele, who had been one of the biggest stars when rock and roll was the latest craze ,just before the Beetles arrived on the scene. He went on to star in a number of very successful films in England and Hollywood, including *HALF A SIXPENCE* which ran on stage for several years and was then successfully filmed with Tommy as its main star. A formidable achievement for a young man who had started his career as a ship's steward. Tommy had avoided television chat shows, until he saw our Niven programme. He liked it so much he agreed to let us make him the subject of one of our programmes. The results surprised him and almost everyone else. He proved to be an excellent raconteur and came across as an extremely talented and very nice man. He had worked closely with Walt Disney and got to know him well. In in our programme he explained how that had come about. He also described the last days of the Warner Brothers empire and a lunch he had attended on Jack Warner's last day in charge of the business he and his brothers had built up. All riveting stuff, which we were able to capture for posterity.

We produced the television programme I enjoyed making most of all shortly after our Niven programme had been released. It featured a friend of his who had served with him during the second world war, When Niven was leading his men into battle as a Sandhurst trained Army Officer, another actor, who had been obliged to join the army when war broke out, was made his Batman. Unlike David, who quite enjoyed his military career, the new recruit hated every minute of his . When he first sighed up and was asked which regiment he would like to join his reply set the tone for everything that followed. He had said "The Tank Corps," because if he had to do anything at all he would prefer to go into battle sitting down! As the war progressed, in Niven he found a kindred spirit. When it ended the two men became close friends. That batman was to be the subject of our next film. His name was Peter Ustinov.

In 1973, when we made our programmes Niven and Ustinov were both at the height of their careers. Ustinov went on to write, direct and star in over sixty operas, films and plays. When he died in 2004 the world lost many irreplaceable talents, some of which fortunately we had been able to capture on film when he was at his best. Peter first appeared on stage when he was 18 years old. He wrote and performed a comic sketch at the Players Theatre Club in London. It was based on a colonial Bishop who had been invited to preach at Westminster school, where Peter's father had sent him to acquire "a traditional English public school education." As he was no good at games and not considered to be academically bright, he started to write plays in school exercise books. The Players Theatre sketch demonstrated his skills as a writer and actor, but they were talents his school always managed to miss. His last end of term report said that he "shows great originality which must be curbed at all costs." In our film, Peter once again became Bishop of Limppopo Land, bringing to life the role which had launched his career when he had just left school. I first met Peter at the United Nations building in Geneva. I think David Niven had already told him what to expect but he did not seem to be have been put off! In the weeks that followed we became good friends, united by two qualities we seemed to share - an ability to get on with all sort of people, and a love of making films.

A you may know the United Nations building in Geneva is vast. Walking at quite a brisk pace it took us about half an hour to walk from one end of it to the other. As we moved along,Peter was approached by a number of people. He, of course, was known by everyone so there was no escape. On each occasion he spoke to them, switching effortlessly from language to language and in some cases from dialect to dialect, greeting friends and telling jokes. It was a walk I shall never forget and there was much more to come.

I had spent two months doing some research. If you are to to be a film Producer and want to make programmes like the ones we are discussing here, you will find that one of the the keys to a successful outcome lies in doing a lot of research. You must know all about the subject you are proposing to film before you start. That means reading everything you can find which has been written by or about the subject of your programme and talking to as many people as a you can who might know more. And don't believe all you read or hear. Check your facts. Well known people often have P r e s s Officers and Agents, who sometimes issue misleading information to boost the images of those they are paid to support. Doing research is hard work but it pays off every time. When Peter and I sat down in front of the cameras for the first time, I knew enough about his life to be able to prompt him to talk about subjects I knew we could illustrate and was sure he would be happy to discuss. My research had unearthed a number of subjects which encouraged him to tell us some wonderful stories on subjects he rarely discussed with anyone.

We shot much of our film on location at one of Peter's homes at Puerto Andratx in Majorca. For two days we sat in his garden and chatted about a list of subjects I had explored in my research. We were also able to film his pride and joy-a very rare Hispano Suiza car. Only a few had ever been built. Alas that one no longer exists. It was stolen shortly after our film was made and, as far as I am aware, has not been seen since. Again we used two cameras running continuously side by side, Sound was recorded on a number of linked Nagra tape recorders set up nearby. We had two of the best Cameramen around. John Alcott, who shot many of Stanley Kubrick's films including *CLOCKWORK ORANGE* and *BARRY LYNDON* looked after camera number one. Peter Duke - a senior BBC cameraman with a wealth of experience, looked after camera number two and was also a joy to work with. Our sound man was David Jones who had started his career with us and always did an excellent job.

When our film was finished, after two months in the cutting rooms, I asked Ustinov if he would like to see it when he was next in London. He said he would and eventually arrived at our offices in Covent Garden. He sat without moving a muscle through the whole of the original sixty minute version. I was beginning to wonder if he had fallen asleep but he had not. When the film ended he suggested we should go to a local restaurant which was famous for the quality of its food to celebrate its completion. In the course of that meal he was kind enough to pay me one of the nicest compliments I have ever received. He said had made lots of of what he described as "instantly forgettable films" but he thought the one he had just seen had probably shown him as he really was. He said he had enjoyed seeing some of the pictures we had unearthed in our research. He also like the shots I had persuaded Westminster school to allow us to film in an attempt to show what the school had been like when he was there. Most important of all to us was the fact that he was obviously happy with what we had done and that meant a lot.

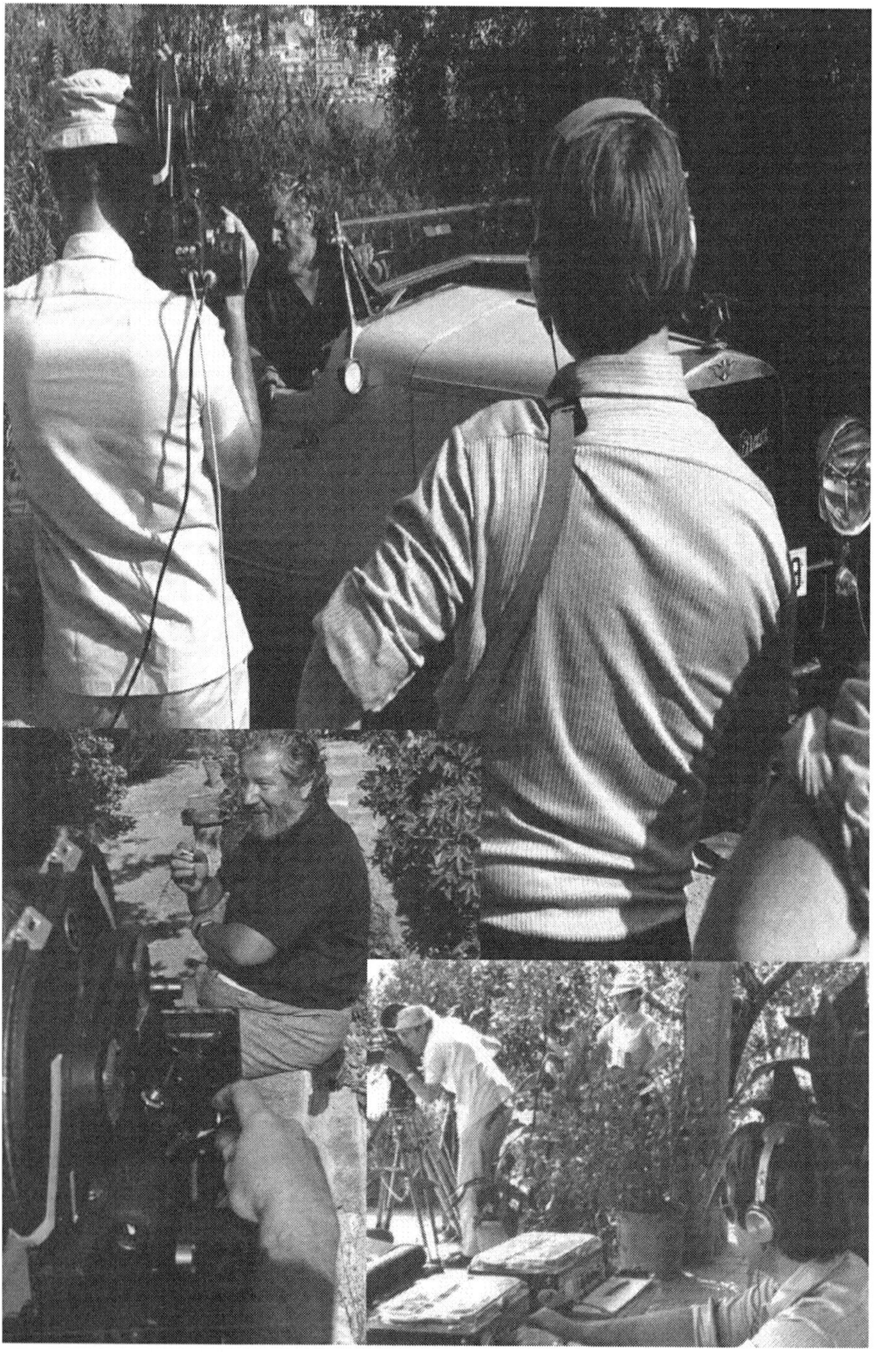

A few years later our original film was lost when the laboratory which had processed it was sold for redevelopment. We thought it had gone for ever but copies have since been found and they have now been digitally re-mastered and restored. As a result. Peter's wonderful performance, (which some have said is the best television programme he ever made) can still be enjoyed and his many talents preserved for future generations.

We made one more television programme that year and then had to turn our attention to the ever increasing number of requests we were getting to make promotional and training films for sponsors who wanted to work with us. For out last entertainment programme we decided to feature a big American star. Though we knew that ,with a one off programme, we had no chance whatever of making any impact on the American television market, we felt that it might be an idea to try something new. The subject we chose to explore was a an actor who was well known in the UK and indeed in much of the rest of the world where he was generally regarded as the king of horror movies. He, of course, was Vincent Price. When I started doing my research I immediately realised that it was going to be expensive and difficult to make a really comprehensive film on a man who was so busy and spent most of his time in the USA. What could we do to interest his millions of fans? I thought that, if we could show what their idol was like, without the horrific makeup he often had to wear, and hear his own views on his career, they would be interested enough to watch. Fortunately that assumption proved to be correct. Again I did not want to make it a film clip show, though on this occasion we did include a short excerpt from from one of his films. As shooting at Price's home in the USA would have been too expensive to consider, I had to find a location where we could film which would be relevant to his career. I eventually chose the Royal Pavilion in Brighton. Vincent had made his stage debut playing the Prince Regent, so that was one obvious connection. As our programme revealed, off stage he was also an acknowledged expert on fine works of art and and an accomplished gourmet cook.

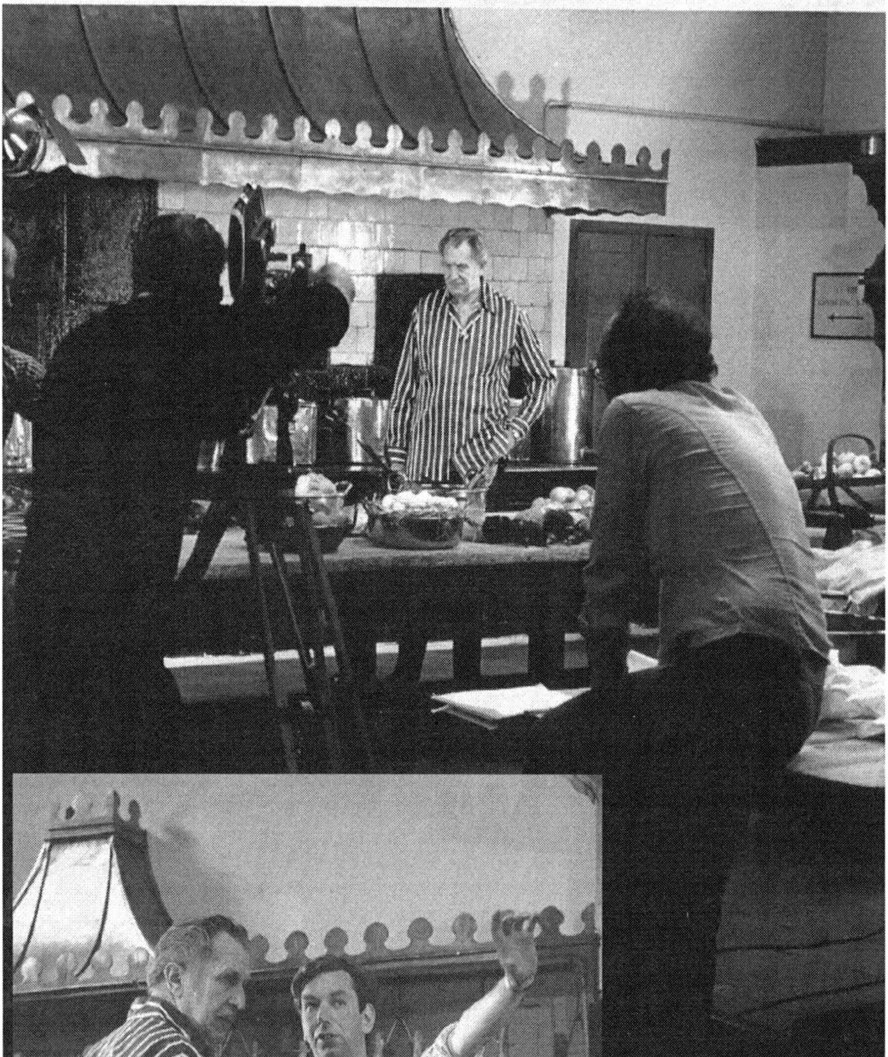

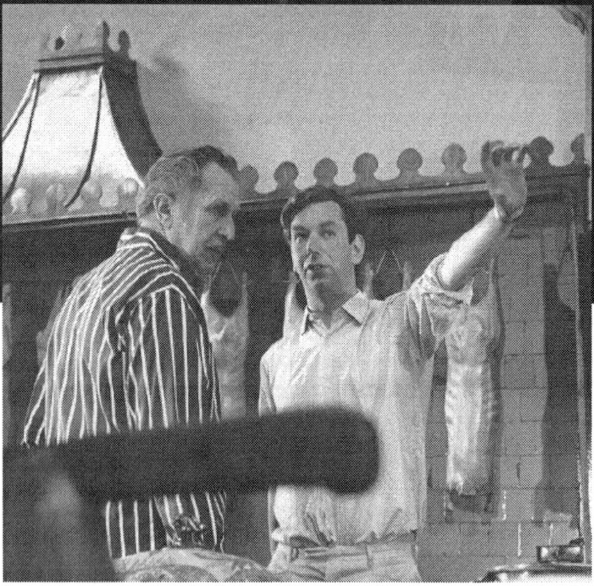

For two days we toured the building and chatted abut Vincent's extraordinary career. Though now principally remembered for his horror film work, he had distinguished himself in several other areas. As a young man he had be awarded a degree in the history of art at Yale University and then a degree in fine arts at the University of London. He went on to start and run a fine art department for Sears Roebuck - one of Americas largest and most successful companies. There he selected and commissioned works for sale to the American public. His purchases included works by Rembrandt, Salvador Dali and Picasso. He was also an accomplished gourmet chef and the author of number of best selling cookbooks so in the kitchens of the Royal Pavilion he was quite at home.

When our film was finished it was generally well received but I have never been entirely happy with the end result. I would have liked more time to spend on it. Alas that was not to be, for in London we had an ever growing list of people wanting us to make promotional and training films with us and some of them were not going to wait.

For our next assignment we turned to crime. When you start your career as a film Producer, if anyone tells you crime doesn't pay do not believe them! It paid very well for us and, in case you want to know how, I will tell you what we did. I became a shoplifter! Before you call the police and have me arrested I had better explain how that came to be. When we got back from our Vincent Price endeavours. I found a letter from a large department store group was waiting for me. It explained that they had a problem and were wondering if we could help. Would I go and see them and hear what they had to say. I accepted their invitation and set out to enter an entirely new world. Like everyone else, I knew shoplifting in London and elsewhere was a big problem. I did not appreciate how big that problem was. My department store contact, who was Head of Security, put me right on that one. What I had always assumed added up to a few high value items going missing each month was, I was told, was a highly organised business which cost his company millions of pounds a year. He then explained how shoplifters work in organised gangs and what they do. Would I be interested in helping to combat their efforts?

In the weeks that followed I learned how to be an expert shoplifter. As mentioned earlier in this book, as a film Producer you rarely do the same job twice. Acquiring new skills if par for the course but this was an unusual move for me and I was quickly hooked. My Security Manager friend showed me the results of some research they had carried out in the last six months. They had installed cameras at strategic points in some of their stores. He showed me what they had witnessed and recorded. He then ran the tapes again and drew my attention to points I had not noticed on my first viewing. "Watch their eyes", he said and then he showed me pictures of the leaders of the gangs they had learned to recognise over the last few moths. Watch that guy in the suit and tie and you will see he doesn't miss a trick," I watched and noticed how the man he had pointed out was constantly looking round. " Now watch that girl over there. The one with the pram". The camera had swung round at that point to show an attractive young lady with a baby in a pram. As I watched she looked round as the man in the previous shot had done. She then leant forward, lifted a cover on the pram, grabbed a pile of jeans from a nearby rack and hid them inside. She checked to make sure no one was watching and then moved on, as if she was just another mother with a child in a pram.

" That young lady costs us thousands of pounds a week. At least she did. We got her in the end, but there are many more who are still at it and they use a variety of techniques."

In the days that followed I learned what those techniques were. We had agreed to make a film to help train staff in stores where goods were being stolen every day. " We have got to stop them chatting and encourage them to watch the eyes and hands of innocent looking customers who are not always as innocent as they appear to be.

I did my homework and gradually acquired the knowledge I needed to make a film which I felt would work. We signed a contract, I wrote a script and our production began. It was so successful that we were asked to make two more films.

In our film we restaged a number of thefts which had taken place in recent months. At the start of the film we told our audiences that in the next few minutes they would see an ordinary day's shopping in one of their stores. We asked them to watch carefully and see if they could spot anything remiss. It took about ten minutes to run those scenes, which were presented in a completely straight way without comment. We then paused and told our audiences that there were a number of things they should not have missed. Getting audiences involved is important when you are making any film and we now had the full attention of everyone who had seen the start of our film. We went on to explain that, if they had been looking in the right places and known what to look for, they could have spotted shoplifters at work in situations which had subsequently landed them in court. We then ran the scenes again and pointed out what they had missed. We drew attention to staff who were chatting and missed what was going on. We then showed what they should have been looking at what they might have missed.

PREVENTING SHOPLIFTING was the title of our film. We made a special version for the store management which was tailor made for them and a general version for release as one of our *COMMON SENSE GUIDE* series. Both did well and lead to our being asked to make a film on credit card fraud and another one for them. They were happy to accept my ideas and gave us a good budget to work with,which proved to be a good move for us and for them. It took me a month to come up with the idea which we and they both thought was best.

On this occasion I again decided to use actors but the treatment I proposed was quite different to what we had done before. This time we would tell a story, again based on facts but we would do it in a very different way. We would see our storyteller in the opening scenes. An ordinary looking man with a cockney accent who seems to ooze confidence and charm, but is basically a crook. His name is Jack and he runs a gang of shoplifters who operate all over town. Jack speaks to our audience as if he was chatting confidentially to a friend and tells them about his life.

Jack is very proud of his team. They're "the best in the business" and they are doing so well he can sit back and relax. His pride and joy is Sally ("Our Sal") an attractive young lady who he has recruited and taught. As Jack confides to our audience, she knows everything there is to know about shoplifting. What to look for. Where to find it, and when to strike. As the film gets underway we watch Sal at work and see what she does. As Jack tells us in his confidential comments, we might not notice anything wrong because " Sal is no fool. She takes her time. She looks for Assistants who are busy chatting, for alarms which are not switched on and goods near exits, all of which are an invitation to crime." In a couple of minutes we begin to understand why Sal does so well. When As Jack's story ends we join Sally as she heads back to join him at the end of her day. She has done well today. Six watches, a carriage clock and cash from an unattended till are just part of her haul. Our camera tracks with her as she returns to Jack's house to pass on her spoils. She rings the door bell and, as usual Jack appears. "Hello Sal", he says and then he steps back. The camera pulls back to show she is in accompanied by two policeman who stand on either side. Sal hands over her bags but not to Jack. The camera pans down to reveal the handcuffs he now wears.

That film, which was called WHAT DO THEY TAKE YOU FOR? was an instant success and it is still popular today. Though it was produced over thirty years ago and the clothes an settings are rather dated, the message it conveys is as clear and important now as it was when it was made.

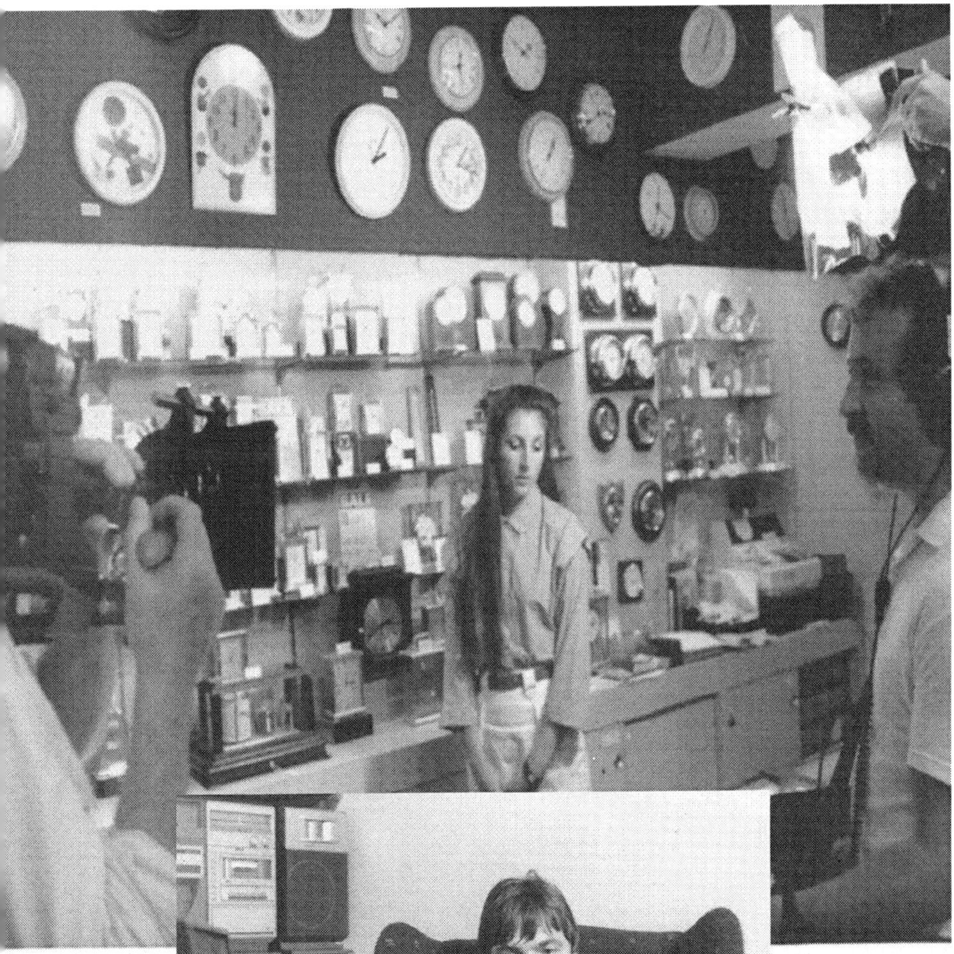

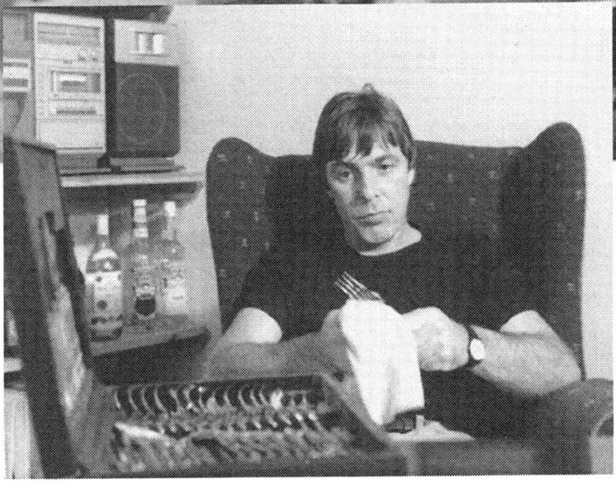

My career in crime was to last a little longer than I originally thought it would. Impressed by our efforts so far we were approached by the organisation which speaks for most of Britain's major insurance companies. The British Insurance Association as it was called then, is an excellent organisation which regulates and speaks for British Insurers. They wanted us to make a crime prevention film and were looking for ideas. I wrote a script which they seemed to like and what was eventually called *STOP THIEF*" went into production. It was a film about burglaries in homes and we staged a number of incidents using actors in stead of the real life people who had actually been involved inn the incidents on which our script was based.

The film worked out well, just as we had hoped it would. It went on to win several awards one of which I was presented with by the man who was then Home Secretary and Deputy Prime Minister - William Whitelaw. I enjoyed making *STOP THIEF!* and working with the ABI. As often happens, when one a film succeeds, people want more. In the months that followed we made several more films for the insurance industry. There was only one thing I was not happy with, and that was not due in any way to the sponsors or anyone else who was directly involved. As It upset me at the time and, as it still does, I will tell you what happened. When *STOP THIEF!* was made I was living I London. I had a house which I had moved into when I was working at Lime Grove. It was a nice house in a quiet street where my neighbours had been living happily for many years. When we were shooting *STOP THIEF!* I decided to break one of my cardinal rules, and allow one scene to be shot in my home. I don't usually do that because I know chaotic filming can be. On that occasion I agreed and one shot was duly filmed with no problem at all.

Six months after that film was completed, my house was burgled. I don't think it had anything to do with the film, as other premises in the same area were broken into that day, but there was one issue which did concern me. When we were making the film I had taken advice on the subjects the film was due to explore. Some very experienced insurance experts advised me on the script and I acted on their advice. They said every home should be fitted with a burglar alarm . I already had one of those. They recommended installing metal gates across any windows which might be used as easy access points. I accepted that advice and had them installed. They said valuable items should always be listed with serial numbers or other key features noted alongside. I had spent several days doing that. They also advised that I should photograph valuable items and get them valued for insurance purposes by a suitable qualified local business. Again I did as I was advised.

When the burglary occurred, my alarm did not work though it had only been installed a few months before. We later found out that a cable supplying power to it had been cut. The strong metal gates had been forced out of my wooden window frames with what must have been a very strong crow bar. I was prepared to accept that as I knew that kind of force is hard to prevent What I was not prepared for was what happened a when I claimed for the things I had lost. They included some quite valuable miniature paintings, which had been in my family for three generations. Military Cross medals won by my father in the first war and by my brother in the second, had also gone though I did not discover that until later. When my insurance claim was submitted (the first claim of any kind I had ever made) my insurers appointed a Loss Adjuster. He duly turned up and made a list. I gave him copies of the photographs I had taken and all the facts I possessed. I fought for months to reach a settlement for the replacement of what I had paid to insure for several years. The Loss Adjuster argued every point and finally advised me that, as the items I had insured had been valued by local businesses and not by an expert approved by my insurance company, my claims would not be met in full. I learned another lesson that day, which our film did not convey. Never trust an insurance company unless you read every line of the small print on all the documents they provide when any policy is taken out or renewed. None of the items I lost, including those irreplaceable medals, has ever been traced or returned.

After learning how to be a criminal, I decided it was time to change jobs. This time I was to learn how to be a doctor. By now you will not be surprised to to learn that my new choice of career had something to do with films. The life of a Film Producer is never dull, as I believe I may have mentioned few times before! On this occasion I was approached by an organisation which helps doctors and dentists who run into trouble. It is not a charitable trust but an insurance based organisation . Doctors (and dentists) like all of us, make mistakes from time to time.. When health issues are involved any mistake can prove expensive. In recent years litigation has become rife in all aspects of the law but when we first got involved, prosecuting medical staff for errors which had occurred was fairly rare. Today it happens much more often. The man who first introduced me to this subject was to become one of my best friends. Armond Gwynne had started his professional life as a Dentist during his national service. He spent a few years doing that, got bored and studied to become a Doctor. With a first class brain and a memory to die for, he qualified with honours in a very short time. After working in hospitals for some time, he decided to study law. Again, in a relatively short time. He acquired an immense amount of knowledge. When we we first met, he was advising an organisation which worked on various aspects of medical practice and the law. In the years which followed we worked together on a number of films for audiences of doctors and dentists. It was nice making programmes for audiences who had brains, and we had a lot of fun. Armond advised me on medical practices and the law. I wrote and directed the films and together we somehow managed to make some pretty boring subjects interesting to watch. In case you feel inclined to explore specialist professions in the course of your work as a film Producer you may care to know what happened and how things worked out.

The first subject we decided to make a film about was a subject many might feel was impossible to film. It was certainly not exciting but, as I was soon to learn, it was crucially important for reasons our film had to explore and explain. That subject was what most patients know nothing about but trust implicitly - medical records.

When you go to see a doctor or a dentist or end up in hospital the details of what has taken place are recorded in your medical notes. That is normally fine, providing those notes have been made in an acceptable way. Usually they are but occasionally they are not, and that is what our film set out to explore. When mistakes are made and doctors or dentists end up in court, their medical notes become evidence which can be accessed by all involved.

If they are accurate, clear and easy to read all should be well, but if they are not, there can be a huge price to pay. If the notes are difficult to read, lawyers can have a field day. If a doctor has added a snide comment the situation can be even worse. The doctor who was asked to tell a court why he had written a footnote at the bottom of a page found himself in difficulties when he had to translate what he had written. At the end of his notes he had simply added some capital letters, separated by full stops - T.S.C.K.I.A .G.H.U. When in court he had to explain that meant - "This silly cow knows it all. God help us," the Judge was not impressed!

So how did we make that subject interesting to watch? Dr Gwynne produced some court transcripts of real life incidents while I tried to find a format which would enable us to make the points the film's sponsors wanted to get across. We eventually decided to use actors to play the parts of doctors and dentists who had landed on court as a result of the records they had kept. That worked well but we still needed an opening sequence which would encourage audiences to watch. I got a clue for that by reading the summing up speech a Judge had made in a recent case. He had said the Defendant would have had a stronger case if he had paid more attention to what he had written.

I decided we should start our film in a completely different setting. Our first scene was shot in the open air at a garden fair. We saw five smartly dressed people facing a table which was a few feet away. As the camera moved closer we saw that the table was stacked high with piles of meat pies. A chunky looking man sat nearby slowly munching his way through pie after pie. The next shot revealed a sign displayed above him. It read -

"World Pie Eating Competition." As our audiences watched what was going on a Narrator spoke our film's opening words. " It's a big moment here!," and then he went on "By the end of today this man will or will not have become Pie Eating Champion of The World." A few shots of the man guzzling away came at this point.

The camera then concentrated on the smartly dressed people who were scribbling away as they watched what was going on. Our Narrator explained what they were doing. "The outcome will be decided by the five Judges. Their decision will be final and it will all depend on their written reports."

As the pie eater grabbed another pie the scene changed. We moved from the pie eating competition to the inside of a criminal court. The pie eating judges were replaced by a solemn looking man in a gown and a wig. The camera moved from him to show a Doctor who was facing him across the court. The film's title was superimposed at this point - *FOR THE RECORD*. We can hear the Judge speaking in court as the title appears. "In your notes you recorded that you prescribed a illegible quantity of a drug which was preceded by what might or might not have been a decimal point. Your instructions were not clear. The wrong dose was given and and your patient died. In this case we will be hearing from....."

The film went of to show what had happened and explain how records should be kept. When it was released it was generally welcomed by the audiences of doctors and dentists it was made for.

As has usually been the case in my the course of my career, one film lead to another and I was asked if I could make a film about some of the other problems which at that time were getting the medical profession a bad press.

This time hospital doctors were to be our target audience. As I knew nothing about medicine and had only set foot in a hospital as a visitor once or twice, I thought I ought to do some research. Doctor Gwynne and I again worked together on this project. He provided the medical expertise and I wrote and directed the film.

Armond Gwynne

As I was writing for an audience of Surgeons who were far brighter than I could ever be, thought I ought to find out how they spoke to each other when they were working together in an operating theatre. I knew that some of my friends, who happened to be doctors, generally laughed at the language often used in television programme hospital scenes.

In an attempt to avoid that happening to my script, I arranged to join a Surgeon when he was on duty at one of the hospitals we hoped to involve in our film. I duly arrived and was greeted by the nursing Sister in charge of the operating theatre where my surgeon was due to perform. He was going to do hip replacements that morning and had agreed I could stand alongside and watch him at work. I needed to know what sort of words and technical terms the operating team used when their work was underway. The Sister in charge clearly believed I would pass out at the first sight of blood. So did I, but I did not tell her that. I had always been scared of hospitals and and was by no means convinced I would be able to pass the test. The incision for a hip replacement is huge and blood pours out everywhere until its flow is controlled. Somehow I managed to concentrate on what was being done and soon became fascinated by what was taking place. The surgical team was was so well organised and so totally professional that my innate fear of hospitals disappeared for ever that day. A couple of hours later I was talking to the elderly lady whose hip had been replaced. She was smiling, and alert and as bright as a lark. From a script writing point of view the outcome was not so good. When the operation started the operating team had only talked about cricket. The job they were doing was so routine that they did not need to discuss it. In stead they discussed all their local cricket teams!

Several years later, when I had a heart attack after working too hard for too long, I recalled that day. In the Royal Bournemouth hospital the brilliant Doctor Tarwar inserted five stents into my heart and gave me a new lease of life. In an NHS hospital I knew I had nothing to fear.

I am often asked if I will "come and "talk to people who want to do what you have done." I much prefer to go and listen to what they can tell me. One of the people who asked me that question a few times over the years, was a recent Headmaster of Milton Abbey - my old school. Jonathan Hughes D'Aeth was a brilliant Headmaster who ran the school superbly for many years. He knew all the boys in his care and did everything he could to give them a good start in life. One day he told me there was a boy he would like me to meet. I said I would be happy to hear what he had to say and left it at that. When we did eventually meet it was immediately clear that he was very bright but his headmaster told me that, like us all, he had a problem. He was dyslexic. I did not really know what that meant but I was soon to learn and I am very glad I did because that young man was to teach me a lot. His first name was Guy.

His parents were deeply involved in running a big company. They loved their son and had devoted their lives to looking after him. They had sent him to Milton Abbey as they had been told it was a school which was small enough to care for people who can sometimes find it is hard to cope with the pace of modern life. The Headmaster's call to me showed how right they were. He had a fine record of helping boys and girls with similar problems and I agreed to see if there was anything useful I could do.

Over the next two years I visited the school as often as I could and tried to encourage the young man. I listened to his ideas and introduced him to professional film equipment and production techniques. I showed him what professional film editing is all about and why it is not just a question of "cutting out the bad bits," as amateur movie makers often assume. He learned about doing research and writing scripts - lessons which are never easy and are that much harder if you are dyslexic and have to dictate what you really want to say. When the time came for him to leave school, he said he wanted to make a film he could use to help him to get a place at a university or on a film making course.

He asked me what his film should be about. I told him that was for him to decide. If he was going to be a film Producer he must choose the subjects he filmed and decide how he was going to present them to the audiences he wanted to reach.

We lent him some gear and he took control from that moment on. I heard that he had started making his film but did not know what it was about or how he was getting on. It had to be entirely his work and I was pretty sure that he would do well. He just needed to be given a chance to show what he could do. When he had finished and showed me what he had produced I was lost for words. He had chosen a very difficult subject to film. I knew a bit about it because one of my former BBC colleagues had made a programme for television on a similar subject a few weeks before. Young Guy's production was infinitely better. The subject he had chosen to explore was not an easy one. It was drugs in schools. Milton Abbey did not have a drug problems but a lot of schools did and still do. As a young man, Guy was on the same wavelength as other young people and approached his subject in a way they could follow and understand. Working completely on his own he had discovered that the acknowledged authority on the subject of drugs in schools was a lady Professor at Oxford university. He had approached her for advice and persuaded her to be interviewed. He worked out his questions, conducted the interview and shot it on film. The Professor was clearly interested and impressed and responded with much better answers than most experienced Journalists would ever have got. Guy then shot some other scenes to illustrate the points which arose from the interview and put the whole thing together on a laptop computer. The final result brilliantly achieved what he had set out to do. I was very impressed , and more proud of what Guy had managed to achieve than of anything I have done in the course of my career. I am delighted to report that now, several years later, he is doing well as a full time professional television Producer. No none deserves his success more.

SCREEN TEST

FIND OUT IF

YOU

COULD BE A FILM PRODUCER

If you want to find out if you have the potential to make a living producing films, here is a little test which may help you to find out If you are or are not likely to succeed.

Throughout this book I have mentioned that you will need something to show what you can do if you want to get a job. You don't need expensive gear or piles of cash to find out and show what you can or cannot do.

Just make a short film to showcase your talents.

By short I mean around fifteen minutes. You can choose your own subject and use whatever equipment you have or can borrow or buy without breaking the bank.

In case you are lost for ideas of a subjects to film I am going to suggest three kinds of films you might wish to consider.

OPTION ONE is for those still at school or about to leave.

Make a film about the school you are in

OPTION TWO

Make a film about the area you live in and places of interest nearby

OPTION THREE

My third and final suggestion is designed to encourage you to make a film on any subject you are interested in. As a test exercise I decided to make a short film about one of our local events - the Dorset Steam Fair. It was shot in a few weekends using basic equipment- A Sony HD video home video camcorder, (Model HDR CX410) .

It was edited on a home computer using Magix software which cost around £50.00 .

And it was great fun to do! So why not see what **you** can do.

You might end up with a career as as film Producer!

Before you start

1. Choose a subject you will enjoy making a film about.

2. List the locations you will need to visit

3. Prepare a shooting schedule which will help you ensure you are in the right places at the right times. Look out for interesting events, consider local weather conditions and then make our plans.

4. Shoot everything you need to tell your story. Keep your camera running until everything you want your audiences to see has been properly explored. You can cut when and where you want when you are editing. You will need a lot more shots than you are likely to use in your final version, to make your film interesting to watch.

5. Keep you camera steady and let the action you are filming do the moving for most of the time. Don't drill yourself into the ground panning everywhere time after time. If you must move, pan *with* a subject holding it in frame or move from a starting point , which is itself a nice shot, to another nice shot which you can hold at the end. Endless moving around can be horrible to watch.

6. Record sounds when and where you can. Sounds bring scenes to life. You can add sound effects and music and use them creatively when you edit your film.

7. Shoot your scenes from as many different angles as you can. You need close ups and long shots to make a film work.

8. Shoot all the footage you need when conditions are right and check what you have done before you lave each location.

9. Transfer everything you have shot to your computer and back it up.

10. Make a first assembly edit. Select the scenes and takes you want to use and put them in the order you feel will work. You can then fine cut action and sound adding transitions and titles to make a final version which is pleasant to watch.

GOOD LUCK!

© John Burder 2015

FILMS RECENTLY RESTORED

DRINK AND DRIVE?

FOR FURTHER DETAILS: John Burder Films
E mail burderfilms@aol.com,
Tel. O1202 757237 or Mobile 07950 287039

FILMS RECENTLY RESTORED

THE PERFECT INTRODUCTION TO BASIC FIRE SAFETY

FOR FURTHER DETAILS: John Burder Films
E mail burderfilms@aol.com,
Tel. 01202 757237 or Mobile 07950 287039

FILMS RECENTLY RESTORED

When Coventry cathedral was rebuilt after the war two of the most successful artists based in Britain at that time were commissioned to contribute major works. This recently restored film records their involvement at Coventry and on some of the other projects they were working on when they were at the peak of their careers.

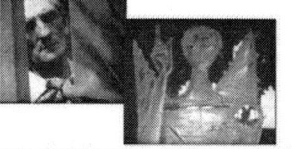

Produced & Directed by JOHN BURDER FILMS
Zone 2 DVD PAL Copyright. ©
E mail - burderfilms@aol.com

Archives 6 GREAT ARTISTS

FROM THE ARCHIVES
Programme 6
GREAT ARTISTS
JOHN PIPER
JOHN HUTTON
20TH CENTURY BRITAIN PRESERVED FOR FUTURE GENERATIONS

THE COMMON SENSE GUIDE TO
MANUAL HANDLING

MAIDEN VOYAGE ON ORIANA

FOR FURTHER DETAILS: John Burder Films
E mail burderfilms@aol.com,
Tel. 01202 757237 or Mobile 07950 287039